Build Your
Dream
Team

Thomasa Bond, EdD

How to
Recruit, Train, and Retain
Early Childhood Staff

Gryphon House
www.gryphonhouse.com

Copyright

© 2020 Thomasa Bond

Published by Gryphon House, Inc.
P. O. Box 10, Lewisville, NC 27023
800.638.0928; 877.638.7576 [fax]

Visit us on the web at www.gryphonhouse.com.

Cover images used under license from Shutterstock.

Library of Congress Control Number:2019957879

Bulk Purchase
Gryphon House books are available for special premiums and sales promotions as well as for fund-raising use. Special editions or book excerpts also can be created to specifications. For details, call 800.638.0928.

Disclaimer
Gryphon House, Inc., cannot be held responsible for damage, mishap, or injury incurred during the use of or because of activities in this book. Appropriate and reasonable caution and adult supervision of children involved in activities and corresponding to the age and capability of each child involved are recommended at all times. Do not leave children unattended at any time. Observe safety and caution at all times.

Build Your Dream Team

TABLE OF CONTENTS

INTRODUCTION

As I was starting to write this book, I was reminded of a time when I was thinking about returning to work after the birth of my second child. I wanted to work only part-time, preferably when my children were taking their naps. I decided to start looking for a job, so I took out the Yellow Pages and started searching for child-care centers located in my area. (For anyone not familiar with the Yellow Pages: It is a book with actual yellow pages, filled with the names, addresses, and advertisements for businesses.) Oh, did I forget to mention I did not want to travel more than twenty minutes from my home? Once I located several centers, I started calling, asking if they had openings for part-time employment. I called maybe five centers before one said yes. I scheduled an interview for the following week, and I was offered a teaching position in a school-age child care program working with children before and after school. This position was perfect because I could be home during the day with my children. The person I interviewed with stated that she was happy that I had called inquiring about part-time work because she was worried that she would not be able to find someone willing to work with an out-of-school-time program.

The following school year, the center needed a lead teacher in their toddler classroom. I had decided to return to work full-time, so I applied for and accepted the position. After working as the toddler lead for a year, the program director who had hired me resigned. Eventually, I was promoted to the program director position. I ended up working at the center for five years, and it had all started with me sitting on my couch calling child-care centers from the Yellow Pages.

The days of Yellow Pages searches have come and gone. Now, program directors must search harder and smarter to find qualified employees to work at their centers. I share this story to let you know that anything can be achieved it you are willing to think outside the box to achieve your goals.

Understand that you can have the best building, the most up-to-date, state-of-the-art equipment, and a STEM-based curriculum to meet all of the children's developmental needs. But, the difference between a basic center and a great center is the staff who implement the program.

When you do not have enough staff to maintain the required adult-child ratio, you should not enroll any additional children. Easy fix, right? Well, maybe not. You are in the business of making money, and having children is where the majority of your revenue comes from. A better solution is to hire quality staff who will stay at the center and to hire additional staff who can cover the classrooms as needed. With a developed operating plan, you can ensure there are enough staff to maintain the required adult-child ratio.

Without a well-trained staff to execute the philosophy and vision of the center, you will not have a high-quality program. According to Johnny C. Taylor, Jr., and Gary M. Stern, Jr., authors of *The Trouble with HR: An Insider's Guide to Finding and Keeping the Best Talent*, "If you don't hire the right people—and retain them—you won't be able to devise new products, meet customer needs, and sustain the business." Therefore, to have a successful center, you first have to recruit and hire the right people.

How This Book Is Organized

The following chapters will provide you with the skills and confidence to recruit and hire the right people to build your dream team for your center. You will gain information on implementing effective recruiting and interviewing, hiring and onboarding new staff, and developing a diverse workforce.

In the first section, we will look at effective recruiting and interview techniques. In the second section we will explore new-hire orientation and initial training, as well as ongoing professional development. Then, we will take a look at working with a diverse workforce, handling staff turnover, and retaining the person for the position.

SECTION ONE
Recruiting and Hiring

CHAPTER 1:
RECRUITING

Make Recruiting an Ongoing Priority

Program directors with limited or no human-resource experience are often required to hire staff. As Harry Chambers points out in his book *Finding, Hiring, and Keeping Peak Performers*, being a program director or center manager "does not automatically guarantee that you have the skills to identify talent and ability or to interview, recruit, and retain highly productive people." Most program directors are required to hire staff, despite lacking the necessary skill set to recruit and hire the right people for the jobs. Individuals without the proper training and experience in recruiting and hiring techniques will ultimately revert to their limited knowledge base and gut feelings.

Some program directors think that they can hire new employees based on the way the person makes them feel during the interview. They may say, "I can look someone in the eyes and tell whether they're lying to me or whether they're going to do a good job." Chambers asserts that "hiring by psychic power, relying on instinct and hunch, is a deadly and costly managerial behavior." Furthermore, using the technique of recruiting and hiring individuals based on your gut feeling will not attract the best individual for the position. As Taylor and Stern write, "People matter, and yet people issues, including recruiting and retaining employees, are often put on the back burner. To realize the full potential of your organization, you need to put the right people in place and then develop them to their maximum." Program directors must develop their recruiting and hiring skills. Hiring and retaining the right people will create a better work environment for the staff, resulting in a more productive and profitable center.

According to Chambers, "In the past, recruiting efforts occurred only on an incremental or as-needed basis. If there was a need to fill a position, recruiting began and then was suspended until the next need arose. Today, your search for peak performers is a never-ending journey . . . Even in the absence of immediate need, you must constantly anticipate the needs of tomorrow. The peak performer you hire next year may be the result of a recruiting seed you planted today. You never know when exceptional candidates will emerge and present opportunities for unexpected growth or organizational upgrade." Recruiting and hiring new employees is not a one-time occurrence; it has to be an ongoing process and recognized as an important part of doing business.

Set aside funds in your budget for recruiting. The recruiting budget should be based on the type of recruiting that you are going to implement. For example, recruiting events will cost more than just posting a job opening on the center's website. Therefore, the amount that is budgeted should be flexible to meet the needs of the center. The recruiting budget may start off small and increase as the center grows. It is important to have a line item in the budget for recruiting so that when the time arises, the center has the funds to recruit for new employees. Chambers asserts, "Recruiting is an expensive task. You must invest wisely in your efforts. Pursuing unfertile areas can waste significant dollars; effective recruiting can be conducted cost effectively if it is well planned." Effective, ongoing recruiting is worth the expense. Evaluate your recruitment budget regularly to ensure that the funds are being used in the most productive way. Decide whether your efforts are generating the results that you want or if a new direction is needed to recruit new employees. Know your job market. Consider, for example, the compensation package you are offering in light of what the job market is looking for. Julia McGovern and Susan Shelly, authors of *The Happy Employee: 101 Ways for Managers to Attract, Retain, and Inspire the Best and Brightest*, suggest, "When looking to attract and hire hard-to-find employees, you have to consider not only what you're looking for but what they are looking for as well. Every person who applies for a job brings with them their own needs and circumstances. When working to hire for hard-to-fill positions, you should consider the circumstances of applicants and what might serve as incentives to get them on board." For example, the pay scale may be fixed, which would make additional incentives beneficial when recruiting new hires for the center. Incentives such as a signing bonus of $75.00 or $100.00 can make a difference. The signing bonus can also be incremental, depending on the position. Twenty-five dollars a year could be allocated for teachers each quarter as a bonus, so that at the end of the first year they would receive a total of $100.00. Distributing the funds quarterly will potentially increase retention, and money will not be given to individuals who leave the center after they receive the signing bonus. If you choose not to have the signing bonus distributed over the course of one year, then anyone who receives the signing bonus must sign a contract for a minimum of one year of employment. If they leave or are fired due to their actions within the first year, they will be required to return the signing bonus. Additional vacation days or personal time off (PTO) can also be an incentive for individuals who have years of experience or an advanced degree. Dominic Cooper, Ivan Robertson, and Gordon Tinline, authors of *Recruitment and Selection*, emphasize both quality and quantity, urging organizations to attract as large a field of suitably qualified and experienced applicants as possible.

Finding Suitable Candidates

Before the program director can hire the right person for the center, an appropriate recruiting process must already be in place. This recruiting process, including word of mouth, should promote the center as a great place to work. Maintain a list of individuals you can contact when there is an opening, and let the current employees know that they can refer friends and acquaintances to apply for open positions at the center. Place open positions on social-media sites. Have a place on the center's website where candidates can apply for positions and post their résumés. Develop a relationship with professors at local colleges and universities, online-program professors, and teachers at the local high school. The recruiting process will also depend on the position that you are trying to fill. If you are looking for a teacher, the recruiting process will focus more in the direction of universities or colleges and websites for professionals. If you are looking for assistant caregivers, these candidates can have less training and experience in most cases. Therefore, the recruiting process for assistant teachers can be directed toward high school and undergraduate college students. Program directors must target the population with the skill set that they are looking for.

Identify the exact skills that you are seeking so that when the job is posted, it will list the specific qualifications required.

Program directors should be continuously recruiting for new employees to work at the center. As Cooper, Robertson, and Tinline point out, "Word of mouth is still an important means for finding new staff and is still frequently used by those seeking work." McGovern and Shelly recommend using conferences, meetings, and professional societies, as these are great resources for identifying potential candidates, as well as terrific places to promote your company. Promote your center as a great place to work and explain why. Provide the reasons why working for your center would be beneficial for a candidate's career. "The key is to get your company's name out there in a positive way, so that people want to work for you," say McGovern and Shelly. Recruitment will not work unless you are networking with others within the field, which is why "Your networking activities should never cease," Chambers asserts. "Become known as a reference point that people can use when they learn of others who may be seeking employment. Do not expect this to be a one-time activity; you must constantly be renewing and replenishing your network sources." Keep a list of names and contact information for potential candidates. Maintain a list of job fairs and contact information for college and university recruitment advisors and local professional groups that you can reach out to when looking for a candidate.

Develop a connection with a local recruiting firm that serves your area. The firm may not represent early childhood professionals; however, you can provide them with the opportunity to expand their clientele by providing qualified candidates for your center. Contact your local high schools and offer the center as a place for the students to complete volunteer hours. Sunny Fader and Angela Erickson, authors of *365 Ideas for Recruiting, Retaining, Motivating, and Rewarding Your Volunteers*, suggest, "Recruiting is the key to effective volunteer programs, because how you recruit your volunteers affects the kind of relationship you are going to have with them." Inviting and supporting volunteer involvement provides the opportunity for the center to be a part of the community, and it will look good on a student's college application. What better way to promote your program than by having students from the community working at the center? Also, retirees with an early childhood background may want to work part time and in some cases full time. Having a trained professional working at the center can potentially reduce the amount of training required.

Connect with local community colleges and universities, and develop internship opportunities for the students at the center. Visit the campuses to meet the professors and teaching staff. This will allow you the opportunity to promote your center as a quality place for students to learn how to interact with children and will help you find students who can work various hours when needed, either part time or as floaters. Once you have developed a connection with the professors at these colleges and universities, offer the center as a learning environment for the students. This will give them the opportunity to volunteer at the center and to complete their required observations of the children and the staff interactions. Ask the professors to provide you with feedback, both on areas where improvements are needed within the program and on things that are working well. This unbiased assessment of your program will be beneficial for staff development and the overall growth of the center.

Many online programs offer early childhood certificates and degrees. Reach out to these programs and offer your center as a practicum location for students in their programs. Many students take online courses through colleges and universities that are not local to them and thus do not have child-care centers for the students to receive hands-on training and experience. Therefore, if you provide a partnership, the institution will have a center where it can send the students for observation and hands-on training. This will provide you with the opportunity to work with teachers who are new to the field and eager to learn.

Training and promoting staff from within the center is an option that should be used whenever possible. Before the students have completed a child-development program, you can hire them as assistant teachers because they are taking early childhood or child-development courses. Allow them to work at the center; once they have completed their education, you will have a qualified staff member who can fill a lead-teacher position when one becomes available. This is the ideal situation for both the center and the assistant.

The center will not have to recruit and train a new lead teacher because a current assistant teacher already meets the requirements. Recognize that parents do not like change, and if the staff member is familiar with the children and the families, it makes for a smoother transition.

It is also a good idea to advertise your center on social media and local early childhood sites. Advertising on social-media sites can promote awareness of the center and provide the opportunity for interested candidates to learn valuable information about the program. The more individuals learn about the program, the higher the chances are that they will apply for a position at the center. Offer a location on your website for interested candidates to upload their résumés. This will provide you with an ongoing list of interested individuals, and you can review their qualifications at your leisure. This form of recruitment does not require a lot of time or effort on your part, and the benefit could be greater if you find a qualified candidate.

Place job postings at local community centers. There could be individuals who are interested in working at your center but do not know how to apply for a position.

Have an open house for applicants to come into your center when it is closed (without children). This way you can show off the center and provide an opportunity for candidates to see firsthand what the program is all about before they apply for a position. You can screen the candidates during the open house and invite the individuals who make it through that first screening to come back for a formal interview. The open house would be the perfect time for your current staff to mingle with the candidates as they are viewing the center. Each classroom could have a staff member who asks different informal questions to determine attendees' skill sets. The candidates should bring their résumés and copies of their unofficial transcripts for review. Reviewing the transcripts will allow you to determine which candidates meet the requirements before you invite them for an official interview.

Consider offering a monetary incentive, such as a bonus, for employees and recruiting connections who recommend an applicant who is ultimately hired. "The best resources for identifying and recruiting job candidates often are right in front of you. Your own employees can be great sources of referrals," say McGovern and Shelly. The thinking is that employees will not recommend anyone who they do not feel is a good fit for the position. McGovern and Shelly point out that most employees are careful with their referrals because they don't want to recommend an employee who would potentially reflect poorly on themselves. "Employees hired through an employee referral program are likely to succeed because their education tends to be similar to that of existing employees and they tend to have similar work ethics, helping them blend with the team culture," McGovern and Shelly advise. When using friends of friends as references, be sure to complete the same screening process you would for any applicant, to ensure that the candidate is a good fit for the center. Also, make sure that the employee and new hire work independently of each other. They are not a package deal; they are individual employees. If one of them is having an issue, it should be clear that the other one is not directly involved.

If you are having a hard time locating and securing lead teachers to work at your center, consider hiring an assistant program director with the qualifications. Sometimes you can attract more qualified candidates based on the advanced title of the position. With this hiring approach, you will have a qualified lead caregiver who can function in two positions. The assistant program director can work in a classroom as a lead caregiver part of the day and work as the assistant for the remainder of the day. When a lead teacher leaves the center, the assistant program director can also cover in the classroom until a replacement can be located or an assistant teacher becomes qualified. Either way, the center will be covered, and the children and parents will not have to adjust to a new person in the classroom. Make sure that the applicants are aware that part of their duties at the center will require teaching in the classroom.

Sharing Employees

Sometimes program directors may have to find creative ways to attract quality staff to work at their centers. "If the perfect candidate doesn't sail through your doors on [the] very first try, ace the interview, and proceed to excel in the position, there are ways to make your own luck when searching for an employee. Consider setting up a training program within your organization," McGovern and Shelly suggest. Create a floater pool for substitute teachers and assistants. Centers can place individuals in a pool that is shared among multiple centers. This way, when you need someone to work for a short period of time, you will have a resource for temporary staff. This pool will also be a useful resource when you are looking for lead teachers, because you have had previous interactions with these individuals. This will reduce the amount of additional training that the lead teacher will require before starting to work in a full-time position. If you are having a hard time finding assistant teachers who are looking for part-time employment, find another center nearby, and partner with them to share employees. Choose your partners carefully. You want to work with a center that has the same work ethic and focus on quality that you do. The center should monitor staff activities to ensure the quality of care being provided. This can serve multiple purposes because the expectation and training of the teachers will be consistent.

You may be thinking, why would I want to partner with my competition? Think of it this way: When we operate as an island and refuse to share ideas and resources that will benefit children and families, that is just wrong. All children should have the opportunity to have access to quality care. If your center is excelling with enrollment, then helping another center that is struggling would benefit the children and not reduce your bottom line at all. Remember that the overall goal within the early childhood field is for all children to have access to quality care within a developmentally appropriate learning environment. Whenever possible, partner with centers that you have visited to ensure that they operate in the same fashion as your center.

Assistant teachers working within the program could potentially work more hours than one center would be able to provide. If an employee is looking for full-time employment, working at multiple locations can provide those hours. This can also provide the opportunity for you to hire individuals who are in the floater pool when an opening becomes available at your center. This approach offers you a chance to interact with an individual to determine if she would be a good fit for your center. If a full-time position becomes available at either center, the center that recruited the employee should have first hiring rights. However, the employee may also choose to work at one center over another. The employee and the centers should be comfortable with this decision. An employee should not be judged based on her decision to work at one center or another, if this occurs.

A Word about Stopgap Hiring

Have you ever started a job and, after a short period of time, noticed that the dependable people are constantly quitting and the unreliable people are staying? Have you ever hired someone to be a warm body for a teacher position, because you could not find a better candidate or you needed an additional staff member to maintain the adult-child ratio? According to Taylor and Stern, "Despite all the lip service given that people are our most important asset, hiring a new employee is often done using what I like to call the stopgap approach. *Stopgap* means plug the leak as quickly as possible. Get the résumés, see who fits the job, interview, and hire." Taylor and Stern warn, "Just doing hiring when someone leaves a job is like putting a Band-Aid on an infection. It won't solve the problem. Companies that hire in an emergency because they are desperate to fill a vacancy are likely to have someone last more than a year about 25 percent of the time."

Be prepared to fill a vacant position at your center by continually recruiting and having a hiring process in place. Whenever possible, hire part-time staff to work as floaters to fill in when needed. The part-time employee can see whether the center is a good fit for her, and you can promote an employee from part time to full time without having to recruit and train a new person. The end goal, of course, is to bring in employees who will fit in and will remain at the center.

Writing a Job Description

The more precise the job description is, the easier it will be to know whether an applicant meets the requirements. "Your job description will define the requirements, your salary schedule will determine the compensation available, and your mission statement will help you and prospective employees determine if their goals and philosophy are consistent with those of the program so that you hire the best possible candidate," Hilda Reno, Janet Stutzman, and Judy Zimmerman, authors of *Handbook for Early Childhood Administrators*, advise. If you want the applicants to be proficient in a certain curriculum, then list that in the job description. If you would like them to work in the infant classroom, then make that a part of the job description as well.

Early childhood centers are becoming more diverse, and they are faced with the challenge of creating a diverse workforce. "People from different cultures do not only look or sound different, they [also] think differently. . . While clear and accurate job descriptions can help all applicants, they can be especially helpful to people coming from different cultures," say Lionel Laroche and Caroline Yang, authors of *Danger and Opportunity: Bridging Culture and Diversity for Competitive Advantage*.

Creating a Job Posting

The posting for the position is a vital part of the selection process. It should be based on the job description and should provide potential candidates with sufficient information to make a decision about whether to apply for the position. When individuals are looking for employment, they should know what position they are applying for; the expectations of the position; and the center's philosophy, mission statement, and curriculum.

The posting for the position should include, at a minimum, the following:

- Title of the position

- Contact person's name and information

- Job description

- Salary range

- How applicants should submit their information

- Minimum and maximum qualifications required

- Workdays and hours

- Projected start date

- Closing date for the position or if the position will be open until an acceptable candidate has been hired

- Any additional requirements, such as proficiency in a language other than English

- The center's mission and philosophy

- The curriculum that is used and how new staff members would be expected to support and promote the curriculum while engaging the children in developmentally appropriate practices

Application Review

When people apply, the program director will want to interview the candidates who meet or exceed their expectations for the position. Generate a list of the qualifications that each candidate should have before she is considered for employment. Be very clear and precise when it comes to what the new hire needs to know coming into the position. Remember that anyone can make herself look good on paper. "Selection criteria are very different from the job description, in that the selection criteria delineate those ideal characteristics that, if possessed by an individual to the fullest extent possible, would ensure the successful performance of the job. Obviously, no one person will possess all the characteristics to the fullest extent, and all characteristics have equal importance in determining who the best candidate is," advise Ronald Rebore and Angela Walmsley, authors of *Recruiting and Retaining Generation Y Teachers*. Create a list of skills that you are willing to train individuals on if they do not have all the requirements for the position. In some cases, you might have a good candidate who does not have all the skills that you require but could be a great addition to the program with some training.

Who will review the résumés? Will they be reviewed by your human resources department (HR), or is this the sole responsibility of the program director? If this is the program director's responsibility, make sure that person has training on the center's hiring policies. Next, decide the criteria by which the individual will be considered or ruled out for the position. (See the Sample Application-Review Form in appendix A on page 88.) Decide if you are going to set your requirements high or use a range for requirements. Consider the following questions:

- How many years of experience working with children in a child-care setting will be required for each position?

- What level of education will be required? For example, would it be acceptable for the candidate to have a bachelor's degree and no experience? Would a candidate who has years of experience and an associate's degree be considered? Which is more important—a degree or years of experience?

Note that there are pros and cons to hiring a candidate based on years of experience. According to Chambers, "When you evaluate experience, you must be aware that you are considering years of positive, valuable experience along with the same years of habitual weakness and bad habits. Just because candidates have done something similar somewhere else does not mean they will meet your objectives for the organization's performance. Hiring experienced mediocrity perpetuates current and future mediocrity. You may be able to relax your requirements for experience if you possess effective skills in coaching or if the organization is capable of training and highly committed to it."

When reviewing the applications, don't be intimidated by an applicant you perceive as being overly qualified and rule her out without allowing her to be interviewed. Recognize that a candidate with more qualifications than you require can be an asset to the center. Just make sure that the center's pay scale is in line with your requirements. If you want to have highly educated and trained lead teachers, plan on paying a fair market wage to these candidates. If you can pay only minimum wage, you should consider recruiting entry-level candidates who have less experience. Remember that the goal is to recruit the best candidate you can afford. If education or training is a requirement for the position, ask candidates to provide an official copy of their transcripts or certificates. Decide whether a candidate has the experience that matches what was provided on their résumés.

Once you have applicants you would like to meet, schedule the interviews. You do not have to wait until the cutoff date for the posting. You want to make sure that you have an opportunity to start interviewing as soon as possible to fill the position.

CHAPTER 2:
The Interview Process

Have you ever hired someone and then wondered, after he started working for you, where the person that you interviewed went? The issue could be because of your interviewing process.

The interview process is where you determine whether a candidate possesses the skill set outlined on his résumé. Use the interview as a time to get to know as much as possible about the candidate's temperament, attitude, and style of handling situations. Recognize that you must have the ability to recruit, interview, and hire individuals who will be committed to the program and the center for a significant period of time.

Consider conducting a telephone interview first. Over the years, I have heard that sometimes candidates do not show up for scheduled in-person interviews. Having a phone interview first can reduce this frustration, because individuals who would not show up for an interview would more than likely not respond to a telephone interview. However, the drawback to screening candidates over the phone, according to Laroche and Yang, is that "there is no opportunity to observe nonverbal cues, phone interviews are very difficult for people who speak English as a second language and may not provide an accurate representation of the candidate's ability to communicate in the workplace."

If you do decide to conduct phone interviews, you'll want to determine whether candidates have the skill set to warrant face-to-face interviews. Again, you should have a ranking system in place to be able to accurately determine the top candidates who will advance to the next level. (See appendix A for an example.) Schedule face-to-face interviews with the candidates who successfully complete a phone interview. Decide how long these interviews will last. Setting a time frame will keep you focused and ensure that all the candidates are interviewed equally. The interview portion should not last longer than one hour.

If the candidate is required to demonstrate his abilities in the classroom, this demonstration can be completed on the same day or scheduled for another day. The candidate should know what to expect from the interview before he arrives. If he is required to go into the classroom, he may dress differently for the interview. Will he be observed during free play, or will he be required to create an activity for the children? The observation should not be completed during a transition period during which the children are leaving the classroom. The classroom observation should not be longer than an hour.

Whenever possible, schedule the interviews when the center is closed, or plan to conduct them at an off-site location. This will reduce the distractions that can occur when you are at the center, allowing you the opportunity to provide your full attention to the candidate during the interview session. "The most important thing you can do while conducting an interview is to give the candidate your undivided attention. You would be appalled, for instance, if a candidate took a phone call during an interview. With that in mind, you shouldn't consider taking a call, either," advise McGovern and Shelly.

A good interview process should include a team of interviewers whenever possible. The program director should have one or two lead teachers and a parent participate in the interviews and hiring selection. "While you may not choose to involve employees in every step of the hiring continuum, they should always have some level of input in selecting new staff members. That input can occur at any point across the continuum of hiring," say McGovern and Shelly. Having a team of interviewers allows you to gather a variety of perspectives. The program director will see the applicant from the perspective of supervision and functioning in the role. A lead teacher will assess whether the candidate can perform the duties and work within the classroom as a part of a team. A parent will evaluate the candidate's ability to work with the children and communicate with families. These are all important areas that a candidate needs to show proficiency in, and having a panel will allow more depth within the interview process. McGovern and Shelly suggest that getting employees involved with hiring invests them in the hiring process, puts everyone on the same page regarding job responsibilities and expectations, makes staff more supportive of a new hire, and increases staff members' willingness to help orient the new hire.

Give each member of the interview team a list of the selection criteria. According to Rebore and Walmsley, this will become a method for quantifying the expert opinions of those who will interview candidates. Without criteria, interviewers are left to their own individual discretion in determining whether an individual will be able to perform the job. Even if you are not able to have an interview panel, make sure that your questions are reflective of all the perspectives needed for the new employee.

McGovern and Shelly suggest setting aside thirty minutes before an interview to review the candidate's résumé and jot down questions specific to his background and experience. Keep a clock in your line of vision so you will know how much time you have left. Candidates tend to get uncomfortable if they see an interviewer checking a watch.

Maintain control of the interview. "Be aware of time. Not only should you start on time, you also should know how you're going to manage your time during the interview so you don't miss any important questions," McGovern and Shelly advise. If you spend most of the time talking about yourself or personal matters not related to the position, then you will hire an individual for the position based more on emotions than on the applicant's actual qualifications. Remember, you are not being interviewed; you are interviewing. Those are different roles. You must allow the candidates to share their knowledge so that you do not inadvertently hire the wrong person for the job.

Keep notes on each of the candidates, even those who are not ultimately selected. You may wish to consider a person for a different position in the future. Also, your notes can help you avoid making the mistake of calling a candidate back in for an interview when you know that the person is not a good fit for your center. According to McGovern and Shelly, "Life is fast, and we're all busy. Keeping track of whom you interview, what you ask, and what they answer is vital. Don't forget to include dates and times of interviews, and keep all your notes for at least a year after making a hire, just in case questions arise down the road."

As you are interviewing the candidates, make sure that you are committed to listening to their answers. Reserve all judgment until all the questions have been asked and answered. Do not fall into the trap of dismissing everything that the candidate says after he says one thing that you do not agree with. Remember, there are many ways to achieve the same result, and the process may be different for each candidate. Candidates do not know the questions that you are going to ask; therefore, if, after a few questions, you find that these candidates are not appropriate for the position and the center, conclude the interview and thank them for coming. Your time is valuable, and you should not waste it on candidates who are not appropriate for the center.

The candidate should not be asked any personal questions such as, "How many children do you have?" "Are you pregnant or planning to have a child soon?" Avoid other topics such as asking the candidate's ethnicity, political views, religious beliefs, or sexual orientation. Be sure to check the labor-relations laws in your state or province to ensure that you are always asking appropriate questions and not violating a candidate's rights.

Establishing Job Expectations

McGovern and Shelly point out that it is important while interviewing to tell candidates what the job will entail and to allow them to ask questions about the position. Employees who are misled during an interview are far more likely to be unhappy in their jobs. Their performance will slip, and before long, they'll be looking for a way out. Taylor and Stern agree, saying, "Interviewers need to be prepared to explain the company's culture, where the new hires will fit into the company, and exactly what is expected of them." McGovern and Shelly also advise that interviewers should "encourage the candidates…to ask questions about the position. If they feel comfortable, you'll be able to get them to ask what's really on their minds. Tackling these questions during the interview is a sure-fire way to make sure there's no confusion on their first day."

Interview Questions

Employees are generally on their best behavior during an interview; therefore, don't expect someone to perform better in the job than he did in the interview. Be prepared with a clear idea of the qualifications and expectations that the candidate must possess for the position. Create a list of questions so that you stay on track. The list will ensure that your questions are asked of each applicant. Document each candidate's answers for each question.

What questions should you ask during the interview? They should directly relate to the duties of the position and be designed to determine whether the candidate has the skills to perform these duties. According to McGovern and Shelly, "You should come up with a rating system that will allow you to judge every candidate using the same criteria and based on the same questions."

Questions on a Candidate's Understanding of Child Development

The interview should include questions that are designed to gain information about a prospective employee's philosophy and understanding of children. I believe that the first question that all candidates should be asked when applying for a position with a child-care center is, "When did you know that you wanted to work in the early childhood field?" If the candidate responds that someone told him that working with children would be an easy job, ask why he sees this as an easy job. This is a crucial point, because it truly takes a great deal of compassion and training to provide children with the quality care that they deserve. Or if the candidate says, "I just love children," ask whether he will love children when they are hitting him and throwing toys. Make sure that the candidates have a true understanding of early childhood development before you hire them to work every day with the children they profess to love. As Sharon Bergen, author of *Early Childhood Staff Orientation Guide*, points out, "Working with children is important, although sometimes an undervalued profession. People who do not understand your work may think it is easy. It is actually complex, mentally challenging, and physically demanding work that requires you to be in top-notch shape to be effective." Taylor and Stern concur: "Establishing the primary motivation for wanting to be hired is critical to determining whether the candidate is a good fit and likely to stay for several years or just turn into another turnover statistic."

Ask questions that will reveal the candidate's understanding of child development and age-appropriate interactions, such as the following:

• How would you handle a child who does not take a nap?

• You have a child who has bitten two children in the classroom. How would you handle that situation with the biter? with the biter's parents? with the bitten children's parents?

• How will you handle a child who cries every day at drop-off?

• How do you respond to a child who does not want to participate in circle time?

• How do you respond to a child who does not want to sit during story time?

• How will you handle children with challenging behaviors (hurting themselves or others, whether physically or with words)?

• What is your transition process?

• What is the adult/child ratio for each age group?

• What are three important rules for the classroom?

• How will you ensure that children are accounted for at all times?

• How important is play? Describe how play will be incorporated into the classroom.

• How do you set up a classroom to eliminate blind spots?

• How will you address children who want to play with the same toy?

Questions on a Candidate's Temperament and Attitude

Candidates' answers can serve as indicators of emotional intelligence, giving you insight into whether they get bent out of shape or take things in stride. You want the interview to be more of a conversation than an inquisition. Taylor and Stern advise, "The key here is asking open-ended questions that will reveal a person's personality and ability to handle conflict, deal with pressures and deadlines, or cope with difficult people on the job." This is the best way to determine which candidate will be the best addition to the center.

Ask questions such as the following:

- A parent is upset because his child is sick, and you called him to pick up the child. How would you handle that situation?

- You have a parent who says her child does not want to come to your class any longer. How do you respond?

- How will you handle the parents who do not want their child to go outside to play?

- How would you handle a parent who is frequently late picking up her child?

- How would you engage a parent who does not speak to you during drop-off or pick-up?

- How would you handle an assistant teacher who is frequently late to work?

- How will you handle the staff member who is not helpful with the children in the classroom?

- How would you address the situation of a parent or staff member who was under the influence at the center?

- How would you address the situation of a coworker who sleeps in the classroom with the children?

- What will you do if you see a coworker being inappropriate with a child?

- How would assessments be completed, and how would that information be communicated to the parents?

- Describe a time when there was an issue on your previous job. What part did you play in the situation? How did you resolve the problem?

- Describe a time when you made a mistake. How did that experience help you grow?

Having candidates describe issues that they have experienced and resolved will allow you to gain a better understanding of how the candidate will handle conflict in the future. How does he describe the situation? Is he eager to place the blame on the other individual, or is he willing to acknowledge the part that he played in the situation? Does he view the situation as a learning experience or as an unnecessary experience? If the candidate views the situation as a growth opportunity, chances are that he has gained the conflict-resolution skills needed for the position. If he views the situation only as a negative experience (which it may have been), then he may not have accepted that all situations can provide an opportunity for personal and professional growth. It is important to hire individuals who have conflict-resolution skills, because this will help them resolve issues that may arise with their coworkers, the parents, the children, and direct supervisors.

If a candidate is unable to see that a situation typically has two sides, then that information can provide insight as to how this candidate will handle situations going forward. Is he the type of person who blames others for his problems? Is he able to work through situations to get to a positive outcome? Can he see how his previous mistakes have helped him to grow? These are all things that you want to know about the candidate before you hire him.

Questions on a Candidate's Professional Expectations and Goals

Have the candidates tell you what they know about the center, along with the qualities they possess that will be beneficial for the center. Ask them to tell you which areas they would need training on to work at the center.

Taylor and Stern say, "Most business managers who aren't trained in hiring ask questions such as, 'Why are you right for this job?' and 'What in your background prepares you for the job?'" They point out that HR experts refer to these as *softball questions*, because they are so open ended that they reveal little about the applicant and whether the person fits the job. Candidates today have many opportunities to develop their interview skills. "In the internet age, company insiders can readily reveal private data about their company's culture, so candidates for jobs are spending as much time evaluating you as you are evaluating them. Generations X and Y . . . are armed with so much internet knowledge that they come to the interview knowing the ins and outs and secrets of most companies," Taylor and Stern add. Therefore, it is important that you do not ask such standard questions as, "Why are you a good candidate for the position?" and "Where do you see yourself in five years?" Instead, ask questions such as the following:

- What goals have you achieved within the past five years?

- What goals have you not achieved, and why?

- What is the one thing that you feel your classroom must have for you to be successful?

- What do you notice about our center?

- Why do you feel this center is a good fit for you?

Ask an applicant for an assistant-teacher position, "Are you willing to go to school to obtain the qualifications necessary to be a lead teacher in the future?" You want to recruit individuals who are willing to become lead qualified, because this will place the center in a better position if a lead teacher leaves. While this should not be a determining factor, it can let you know what a candidate's future at the center might be.

Other Considerations

Observing the Candidate in the Classroom

As part of the interview process, you should have the candidate demonstrate his abilities in the classroom. By so doing, you can see how he interacts with the children. You can see his verbal and nonverbal responses. If a candidate goes into the classroom and does not interact with the children, you cannot expect that he will interact with them once he is hired. It is also important to see how the candidate speaks to the children and the other teachers in the classroom.

Be prepared to pay the candidate for the hours worked during your interview process. The candidate should not work more than one hour in the classroom, and paying him for that hour will be cheaper than hiring the wrong candidate because you did not have the opportunity to observe his interactions before you hired him. As Reno, Stutzman, and Zimmerman point out, "If . . . you decide not to hire, you have effectively required the candidate to work without payment. If you do hire, the person has worked for several hours and deserves compensation." Keep in mind that in some states you cannot have an individual working without compensation. Check the laws in your state before you have a candidate work in the classroom.

If you choose to have the candidate interact with the children, how long will he be evaluated? The candidate should not be evaluated for more than one hour. The candidate also should not be left alone with the children during the observation period; there must be a staff person supervising the candidate during this time. Be sure to inform the candidate about how long the evaluation will be.

Decide what the candidates will be evaluated on during the observation. Candidates do not need to know what they're being evaluated on, but some form of assessment should be used to determine competency levels. Candidates should go into the classroom with the age group that they are applying to work with and should be evaluated on their interactions with the children and their overall behavior in the classroom. Is the candidate making eye contact with the children? Is he at the child's level? Is he speaking in an age-appropriate tone? Is he asking open-ended questions? Is he assisting the children in a way that creates independence, or is he doing everything for them? Is he taking the initiative to interact with the children, or is he waiting for them to approach him?

Ask for a Writing Sample

Have candidates complete a writing sample so you can evaluate their writing proficiency. Determining writing ability is important, because teachers often send notes home to parents, complete bulletin boards, write lesson plans, send out newsletters, and create signs in the classroom for the children, all of which represent the center. These tasks could pose a problem if a candidate does not have proficient writing skills. The person you hire will not just work at the center; he also represents the center.

Wrapping Up the Interview

End the interview with one last question for the candidate: "Is there anything that you feel is important for me to know related to your skill set that has not been previously addressed?" This information will allow the candidate a final opportunity to convince you that he is the best candidate for the position and the center. Remember, the overall goal is to hire the most qualified individual so that he will be successful in the position. Even if you are not planning to offer the position to the candidate, this question can still be the last one asked. With this additional information, you may decide to reinterview the candidate in the future for a different position.

Conclude the interview on a positive note. Each candidate should leave the interview feeling respected. You want each person whom you interview to speak positively about the center and his interactions with you. Remember that word of mouth is still important in the recruiting process.

At the end of the interview, let the candidate know that the selection for the position will be made within the next couple of weeks. McGovern and Shelly state, "It happens to almost all of us at one point or another. You're sure that the candidate you've just finished interviewing is perfect for the job, and you're incredibly tempted to make an offer then and there. Avoid the temptation! Even if you're absolutely convinced that you want to hire this particular candidate, you should end the interview and let them know you'll be getting back to them very soon. Even if you only wait an hour or so, it's a good idea to give yourself some time to assess the situation. Take time to review your notes on all the candidates once more before making a decision."

Evaluating the Candidates

After each candidate has been interviewed, use your post-interview assessment tool (see appendix B on page 89 for a sample) to rank them. This process should be completed immediately after the interview while the candidate's responses are still fresh in your mind. Make sure that you factor this time into your interview process.

Reference Checks

Now that you have narrowed your applicants down to the candidates that you would like to hire, it is time to check their references. "Conducting a reference check does not absolve you of responsibility for an employee's actions," say Reno, Stutzman, and Zimmerman, "but it does reduce the chances of an additional charge of negligence." What types of references will you require? Many centers ask for the following:

- Previous employers and program directors

- Names of coworkers, professors/teachers, or someone who has known the candidate for more than five years

Realize that no one is going to provide a person as a reference who will not give the candidate a glowing recommendation. Therefore, it might be a good idea for one of the references to be from an individual with whom the candidate had a conflict that was resolved with a positive outcome. The benefit of having a coworker as one of the references is that he or she would have worked directly with the candidate. Applicants always try to make themselves look favorable as if they have never had any form of conflict in their entire lives. If we are being truthful, we have all had some form of conflict. It is the growth that comes from conflict resolution that truly defines a person's character. Learning how the candidate handled having issues with a coworker, finding out how they were resolved, and knowing whether the candidate could now work with that coworker tells you how the candidate will respond at your center when conflict arises. Conflict is going to happen, and you want employees who have proper and productive conflict-resolution skills.

Here are some questions to ask the candidates' references:

- Was (candidate) a reliable employee?

- How long did he work at the center?

- What are his strengths?

- What are some areas where he could improve?

- How would you describe his work ethic?

- Would you hire/work with him again?

- How well does he work with children?

- What age group did he work best with? What age group did he work with?

Background Checks

After you have checked the candidates' references, complete a background check. Federal law requires that all states receiving funds from the Child Care Development Block Grant (CCDBG) Act of 2014 have a comprehensive background check completed on anyone employed by a child-care center, as well as on all individuals who have unsupervised contact with children. Federal law also requires all states to have child-care staff and anyone who has unsupervised contact with children to be fingerprinted. The comprehensive check can be completed by an agency that has state approval to complete the background checks. States also require that all individuals working with children be cleared through the state central registry for child abuse and neglect.

The background check should include criminal history and any history of child abuse and/or neglect. If an individual has a criminal history involving children or a history of child abuse and/or neglect, that person should not be allowed to work at the center. The center should also include a clause in the staff handbook that addresses the requirement for employees to be free of accusations and convictions of child abuse and/or neglect. The background checks are important for the safety and well-being of the children. Before the federal law was instituted, some programs completed background checks only for individuals who had direct contact with the children. If background checks are not performed for all staff, you are potentially placing the children at risk. It is better to have complete background checks on all individuals who work at the center, no matter which position they hold.

Taylor and Stern advise, "Don't be fooled by someone who has the right degree, impressive credentials, and all the right skills. If the person can't fit into your culture, all the skills that they possess won't be useful." Chambers asserts, "Often, the wild card in hiring is the key consideration of how candidates will fit in. This is not determining whether you or the people in the department will like the candidates; it is determining whether the candidates will make an effective contribution to the group. Will they bring unique strengths and help overcome existing weaknesses? Will they perform and behave in a manner that promotes . . . harmony? . . . The key consideration is whether candidates will complement the existing environment and find that the existing circumstances meet their needs."

CHAPTER 3:
HIRING

Now that you have completed the interview process, the next step is to make an offer of employment to the candidate you feel will be the best fit for the center and meet the needs of the families and children. Hiring the right staff is putting your recruiting and interviewing steps into action. "When you are hiring new staff, the more work you do before you hire, the easier your job will be after you have chosen a candidate," assert Reno, Stutzman, and Zimmerman. Furthermore, hiring the best candidate is a major step toward building your dream team.

Whenever possible, have at least three candidates whom you would hire for the position. In the event that your first candidate is not willing or able to accept the position, you will have someone else to contact without having to start the process all over again.

The candidate must give notice to her current employer; it is customary to give a two-week notice when leaving a position. Although you may need the employee to start the position sooner, it is important to be respectful of the current employer. Also, you want to be careful of hiring anyone who is willing to leave her current employer without proper notice. The candidate may also do the same thing to you one day.

An important component for building a successful dream team at your center is having qualified and dedicated teachers. The program will thrive or fail based on the performance of the staff hired to work at the center. Therefore, make sure that the individuals you hire have the qualifications and work ethics that you desire. Do not hire an individual who displays qualities that you are not comfortable with. Do not set yourself up for high staff turnover by thinking that you can change or mold an employee's behavior to meet your needs.

At a minimum, qualified lead teachers should meet the qualifications outlined by your state or provincial early education department. In addition, set the education and qualification requirements for new hires at your center; the qualifications that are required by the center can always exceed the state's requirements. One of the requirements should be the individual's dedication to the profession, but dedication may be hard to recognize on a résumé. A dedicated individual will always put the children's safety and well-being first and will have a clear understanding of the importance of developmentally appropriate practices. Just remember that you do not want a lead or assistant teacher working at the center who is not dedicated to the children and the early childhood profession.

Consider and plan for the amount of time needed to supervise and train the individual. Bill Marvin, author of *From Turnover to Teamwork*, says, "When we select people to become part of our staff, it must represent a commitment . . . to do everything possible to encourage and support [a new hire's] development, both personally and professionally. If you are not comfortable making that level of commitment to an individual, you should not bring that person on board." This is where the program director has to assess her time and willingness to invest in the new hire. Program directors should not set themselves or the new hire up for failure with unrealistic expectations. Recognize that the new hire will not be successful if you have not developed a plan to ensure her growth and success.

Hiring Policy and Process

Regardless of the recruiting methods that a program director decides to use, a written hiring process is needed. This is the best way to ensure that everyone in a position of authority is aware of the goals and expectations for the staff. The hiring process should not leave the center when a program director leaves. I have been at several centers with new program directors, and many of them say, "I have no idea what the previous program director did," and "It will take me a few days or weeks to dig through the pile of papers before I can organize the office." Having a written hiring policy will reduce this frustration on the part of a new program director.

Develop a hiring policy that requires the screening, training, and onboarding processes be completed before an individual is hired. In your written hiring policy, define all the requirements for employees before they start working at the center. Include the following requirements for any candidate who is offered employment:

- Official transcript

- A complete physical

- Negative tuberculosis test

- Criminal-history check

- First-aid training; infant and child CPR certification

- Bloodborne pathogens training

- Safe sleep and shaken-baby training

- New-hire orientation before working with the children

Offering Employment

After you have made the final decision about whom you are going to offer a position, contact her and offer her the job. Be sure to include a date by which she must accept or decline the position. McGovern and Shelly warn, "Many candidates have reacted enthusiastically to a phone call saying they were hired only to back out of the arrangement later on, so it's important that you set a date by which a firm decision has to be communicated."

If the candidate accepts the position, send a formal offer letter. McGovern and Shelly advise, "The written offer of employment is important for several reasons. First, it will lay out the terms of employment. Second, it's probably the first written document from you that the candidate has seen, thereby establishing expectations for what is to come." The offer letter should include the following information:

- The job description of the position that the person is being hired for

- The start date and time

- The rate of pay

- The name and contact information of the person the new hire will be reporting to on the first day

- The length of the orientation, training, and observation period

- Any documentation the new hire is required to bring on the first day, such as her driver's license

Once the selection process has been completed and the new hire has accepted the position, send all candidates who were not selected an email or letter informing them that the position has been filled. Candidates appreciate being informed; it is professional to inform them and not leave them waiting and hoping for a position that is no longer available.

Bringing a New Hire on Board

Of course, before you ask someone to come in for an interview, you will have reviewed that person's application. During the interview, you will have learned more about the candidate's qualifications, training and education, experience, attitude and temperament, and understanding of child development and developmentally appropriate practice.

Before you offer a position to a candidate, you will have checked her references. You will also need to conduct a criminal-history check, including a confirmation that there is no history of child abuse and/or neglect. For additional information related to background checks, review the following websites: Child Care Aware of America (https://www.childcareaware.org/background-checks/) and ChildCare.gov (https://www.childcare.gov/consumer-education/background-checks-what-you-need-to-know).

Once you have made the offer of employment to the candidate, have her start the onboarding process. *Onboarding* is completing the required paperwork needed for the candidate to become a part of the center. This can be initiated before the candidate starts working at the center. The new hire can drop the information and forms off at the center or complete online forms at the center's secure website. Having this information completed prior to the official start date will help to expedite the process. "Don't offer an onboarding program that is disorganized, sloppy, or poorly presented," McGovern and Shelly warn.

You want the new employee's first impression of the center to be positive. You don't want her to feel that she has made a mistake in taking the position.

To confirm a candidate's education and training, you will need official copies of all transcripts. Before beginning work, the new hire should have a physical and provide confirmation signed by a licensed physician that she is in good health and able to work with children. You do not want to hire a teacher to work in the infant classroom, for example, only to find out that she can lift only five pounds or less because of a medical condition. Check with your local health department to determine whether employees are required to have a negative tuberculosis test before working with children. Tuberculosis is a highly contagious bacterial infection that is spread through coughing, sneezing, speaking, or singing.

First-aid training and infant and child CPR certification should be required of all staff; state requirements may differ on this matter. The American Red Cross, National Health and Safety Association, and American Heart Association offer a two-year combination course that includes first aid, CPR, and automated external defibrillator (AED) certification training. In addition, all staff must undergo bloodborne pathogens training. The U. S. Occupational Health and Safety Administration (OSHA) requires workers who may come into contact with pathogens present in blood or other bodily fluids and materials to be trained in keeping themselves and others safe from infection. According to OSHA, a *bloodborne pathogen* is a microorganism present in blood or bodily materials that can cause disease in humans, such as the hepatitis B virus, human immunodeficiency virus (HIV), and syphilis. Early childhood teachers and staff regularly come into contact with all sorts of bodily substances. Therefore, this training is very important to keep the children and staff protected from the spread of disease.

Teachers who work with or may work with babies and/or toddlers will need to be trained in safe sleep practices and shaken-baby syndrome. (The only time all staff would not be required to complete this training is if your center does not have infants or toddlers in your care.) All staff should be trained if the center cares for infants, because there is a chance that a teacher may be needed to work in the infant classroom. The American Academy of Pediatrics recommends that all children younger than one year of age be placed on their backs on a firm surface to sleep. Soft bedding, blankets, and pillows should not be used. These practices are intended to prevent sleep-related infant deaths, including sudden infant death syndrome (SIDS), and accidental suffocation or strangulation.

Infants have weak neck muscles. The American Association of Neurological Surgeons warns that shaking a baby can cause serious and sometimes fatal brain injury, including hemorrhaging (bleeding), subdural hematoma (collection of blood on the brain), nerve damage, and irreversible brain damage. All staff should be trained in the dangers of shaking an infant and in methods of prevention.

The new-hire orientation should be a part of the onboarding process. The information to cover in orientation will be discussed in the next section, "Training and Retaining," beginning on page 43.

Observation and Performance Period

Observing the staff is the only way to ensure that they understand and are following the rules of the center. When you observe staff frequently, you will be able to determine whether they are aware of the policies and procedures and whether they are behaving in a fashion that is acceptable. Both positive and negative actions should be addressed immediately. Compliment and support staff members who are performing well; address any negative issues quickly, fairly, and firmly.

Laroche and Yang advise that the program director should explain clearly how performance is measured by using concrete examples to illustrate what good, average, or poor performance looks like. Communicate with the new hire during the observation period so that she is aware of the process and your expectations. Doing so will eliminate the chances of a staff member being surprised at the end of the observation period. This will also reduce mistakes that could potentially place children in harm's way.

New staff should be observed for a period of no less than six months and no more than one year before they become full employees. During this time period, have a clear set of expectations and criteria that the individual is expected to meet or exceed. For example, new hires should do the following:

- Be on time for work

- Interact with the children in a positive and age-appropriate fashion

- Communicate in a positive and constructive fashion with the children, coworkers, and parents

- Incorporate age-appropriate free-play activities

- Ask open-ended questions when engaging the children

- Maintain accurate attendance and know the location of the children at all times by completing a name-to-face check regularly

- Incorporate transition times that are smooth for the children

- Maintain the center's philosophy and mission statement

- Use appropriate discipline with the children by talking to them and redirecting their actions when appropriate

The criteria will help you to determine whether the staff person will be a good fit for the program with additional training.

Allow new hires to accumulate sick and vacation time during the observation period, but do not give them access to paid time off until they have successfully completed the observation period. According to Reno, Stutzman, and Zimmerman, because this is a trial period, it is essential that the program director invest time in evaluation and training to ensure that at the end of the observation period the new employee will be an asset to the program.

During the observation period, the new hire should be aware of what will happen if she has an issue during the specified time frame. Will the observation period be extended? How many infractions are allowed? What events constitute minor issues? What events constitute major issues that would reduce the chances of keeping the new staff member? Rules should be consistent for all employees. The last thing you want is for the employees to compare notes and determine that one was let go and another was kept for the same issue. Being fair and consistent with all employees is not only right; it is also the best way to gain the trust and respect of the staff members.

After the observation period has been completed, the new hire should be evaluated to ensure that she has retained the information that was provided. The evaluation can also be used to ensure that the areas needing correction have been addressed. The evaluation should include a review of information provided in the new-hire orientation. The following are a few of the items that should be addressed during the evaluation:

- Adult-child ratio for each classroom at the center

- Maintaining accurate daily attendance by completing frequent name-to-face checks

- Requirements of emergency procedures

- Licensing rules

- The center's philosophy

- Hours of training required

- Diaper-changing procedures

- Parent communication

The evaluation does not have to be written; it can be a conversation during which the questions are asked to provide clarity if needed. Remember: Without follow-up, you have nothing to ensure that staff members understand the policies and procedures.

Assessing the Effectiveness of Your Recruiting

The program director should regularly review and assess the effectiveness of the recruitment methods that are being used to see what has been working as well as what practices could be improved or removed. The success of the recruitment methods should be based on finding suitable employees for the center. Rebore and Walmsley advise, "Successful and satisfied employees are a good indicator of the quality and success of the marketing and recruitment processes. According to Johnny C. Taylor, Jr., and Gary M. Stern, Jr., authors of *The Trouble with HR: An Insider's Guide to Finding and Keeping the Best*

Talent, "If you keep a staff member for three to five years, you are making a very good return on your recruiting investment. Any time spent at the organization less than that and you've lost money."

Program directors may not view recruiting and hiring as their favorite part of their job function, but it is clearly an important task. According to Alison Barber, author of *Recruiting Employees: Individual and Organizational Perspectives*, "The success of later human-resource efforts, such as selection, training, and compensation, depends in part on the quality and quantity of new employees identified and attracted through the recruitment process." Think about how happy the parents, children, and staff will be when you do hire a great addition to the center and add to your dream team.

SECTION TWO
Training and Retaining

CHAPTER 4:
New-Hire
Orientation

In *Early Childhood Staff Orientation Guide*, Sharon Bergen emphasizes the importance of initial training for new employees. "Newly hired employees are typically enthusiastic and positive about their new situation. However, they may also feel a bit overwhelmed by all the newness—new information, new expectations, and new experiences—coming at them at one time." Orientation will help the new employees learn about the center's requirements before they officially start working with the children. They will be better equipped to work in the classroom and to follow the center's requirements. Bill Marvin advises, "A new hire orientation is an investment that will help you get maximum value from your most precious assets, your staff."

Some program directors may feel that they do not have any extra time to train new hires; this is probably an accurate statement. However, when new employees are not trained, they have a large void in their information pertaining to the center. Without a new-hire orientation, new employees are forced to obtain information only after a mistake has occurred, which is not beneficial for anyone. You can either invest the time on the front end, before a new employee starts, or invest time on the back end after a new hire has been working for a while. The time spent up front completing the orientation can be planned; the time spent correcting and addressing issues cannot be planned and will never be convenient. "There are many ways to plan an orientation, but each has the same objective. The more you can make a new staff member feel valued and important, the more likely he or she will become a long-term mainstay of your program," Reno, Stutzman, and Zimmerman assert.

Tips for a Successful Orientation

Provide the new hire with a schedule of events that will take place on the first few days of orientation. This will let him know what to expect and help him to feel comfortable and welcomed into the center. A well-organized orientation will increase employee retention and reduce staff turnover.

Assign an experienced staff member the role of mentoring the new hire. The mentor will provide the new employee with guidance and support and will help create an environment where the new hire is more likely to succeed. Choose a mentor who will be positive. "The person you choose needs to be a good communicator, must have the time to train and orientate the new employee, and should exemplify the values of the organization," McGovern and Shelly advise. "The new worker is sure to have dozens of questions during the first few weeks, and it's helpful to have a designated 'buddy' to answer them and assist in other ways. The new hire may feel more comfortable approaching a coworker with mundane questions than a manager."

On the first day at the center, have a lunch at which all the staff members have an opportunity to meet the new employee. Having the meet and greet during the lunch period and providing food for everyone will make the team feel a part of the welcoming process. If you have a large center, the meet and greet could be a two-day event so as not to overwhelm the new employee. The mentor should be with the new employee for the meet and greet to make introductions. Because not everyone is comfortable meeting new people, the new hire should not be left alone to make his own introduction to the staff.

The new-hire orientation should not be rushed. Whenever possible, complete the orientation and initial training in short segments over a couple of days. This will allow the new employee an opportunity to absorb the information without being overwhelmed. A one-day orientation will not provide an adequate amount of time to train the new hire to be successful at the center.

Schedule the orientation during a time when the person who is conducting it is not needed for other duties, such as answering the phones or handling staff issues. The trainer should not have to leave the training frequently or abruptly for any reason.

Do not give the new employee a manual to read with the expectation that he will retain all the information contained in it. When someone says that he understands the information, it does not necessarily mean that he truly understands. The training should provide the employee with a review of the employee manual and should allow him time to ask questions.

The best time to complete the initial training is during the new-hire orientation, before the employee begins working directly with the children. This will create a unified atmosphere, with all staff receiving the same information in the same fashion. First impressions are important when the new employee starts working at the center. "If you rush someone onto the job and promise that you will handle their orientation later (when you have a chance), several things may happen. First, you will never get around to the orientation because your life is already a series of crises and there are certain to be more. Second, the new worker will be tossed to the sharks without the support needed to be successful. This increases the likelihood that the worker will make mistakes, develop bad habits, or feel like a failure, any of which can trigger the worker's decision not to stay with the center," Marvin points out. Reno, Stutzman, and Zimmerman add, "If the staff orientation is complete and thorough, there should also be a written acknowledgment that the staff member has read the policies and agrees to abide by them."

Initial Training

Start by determining the new employee's knowledge base. An effective way to do this is to have him take a pretest (see appendix C on page 90) based on the information that you want him to know before working unsupervised with the children. Based on his answers, you will know where to start your training. A pretest ensures that all individuals are aware of the expectations of your center.

After orientation has been completed, have the new hire complete a posttest (the same as the pretest) to assess his understanding of the information you have provided. The pre- and posttests should cover the same information.

The information obtained from the pre- and posttests will also allow you to develop additional training materials. You may also wish to ask the staff members to complete an evaluation after working at the center for two or three months. They can provide feedback on what information would have been beneficial for them to know prior to working in the classroom. This will allow you the opportunity to adjust the training to meet the needs of future hires.

Training Topics

"All new employees, regardless of their education and experience, need to learn the specific policies, practices, and procedures of their new position and program," Bergen says. Provide the new hire with the staff handbook on the first day, and review it with him. Encourage him to read over the staff handbook after the first day and to bring any questions to the second day of the orientation. New hires should receive training on the center's expectations for the position they were hired for. Outline the center's philosophy, the curriculum used by the center, accountability expectations, the chain of command, social-media policies, parent communication expectations, and the center's policies and procedures, so that the new employee has a clear understanding before he starts work.

A well-developed code of conduct will provide clarity and continuity for all employees. The expectations and behaviors should be outlined, along with the consequences of infractions. Your code of conduct should make clear that under no circumstances are staff members to provide inappropriate discipline, either verbally or physically. They are also obligated as mandated reporters to report any form of abuse or neglect to the proper authorities. When the code of conduct is incorporated and followed, employees will instill trust in the parents who use the center. Most employees are hardworking and ethical. However, a small number of employees choose to turn a blind eye to unethical behavior. The unfortunate part is that it only takes one unethical person to taint the perception of the whole center. Reduce unethical behavior with education about the center's expectations as well as the laws of the state or province, and provide training on the state or provincial requirements to ensure compliance. The new hire should also be provided with an organizational chart that outlines the center's chain of command, including communicating with parents. Include topics such as the following in orientation training. Add any others that are specific to your center.

Payroll policies

- Staff sign-in policy

- How staff will be paid (by check or direct deposit)

- Pay frequency (weekly, biweekly, twice a month, monthly)

- How time is reported and to whom

- When the first paycheck will be received

- Policy on loans or advances of monies

Work schedule

- How to change the work schedule

- Break schedule (how long and how many are provided)

- How to schedule days off

- Calling in sick

- Policy for reporting late to work

- Vacation days (how they are accrued)

- Inclement weather policy

Benefits

- Health insurance

- Child care (discounted or free)

- Tuition reimbursement

- Training reimbursement

Mandated reporting

- State or provincial laws on reporting abuse or neglect

- How to report suspected child abuse or neglect

Discipline policy

- Explain what is not allowed with children

- Explain in detail what type of discipline is allowed and expected to be followed with children

Code of conduct

Grounds for immediate termination

- Child abuse

- Child neglect

- Stealing

- Being under the influence of any substance

Dress code

- What is allowed

- What is not allowed

Cell-phone use

- Rules on use in the classroom

- Rules on receiving or making personal calls

- Sharing a personal phone number with parents

Social-media rules

- Being friends with parents on social media

- What can be posted

- What cannot be posted

- Center's website and social-media pages

- Consequences for not following the policies

Maintaining confidentiality

- With coworkers

- With parents

- With children

Parent communication

- What can be discussed with a parent and by whom

- What is not allowed to be discussed with a parent

- Rules on staff providing care for children after the center is closed

- Parent board

- Email threads

Emergency procedures

- Frequency of practice drills (state or provincial requirements)

- Fire

- Natural disaster (tornado, hurricane, mudslide, flooding, ice storm, earthquake)

- Man-made disasters (utility outage or interruption)

- Serious accident (anything from a bump to medical treatment)

- Crisis management (bomb threat, intruder)

- Lost or unsupervised child

Licensing rules specific to your center

- Adult-child ratio

- Daily attendance

- Safe-sleep practices

- Shaken-baby syndrome

- Postings

Organization chart

- Where each employee fits on the chart

- Whom each employee reports to

Job descriptions

- Program director

- Assistant program director

- Lead teacher

- Assistant teacher

Teacher responsibilities

Overall

- Prepare the daily lesson plan

- Supervise the assistant teachers and volunteers in the classroom

- Organize the classroom so that it is age appropriate

- Maintain daily attendance records

- Communicate with parents

- Rules on working in their own child's classroom

Room arrangement

- Developmental areas

- Equipment list (specific items, quantity)

Cleaning requirements

- Daily

- Weekly

- Monthly

Opening procedures

- Expectations of each staff member

Closing procedures

- Expectations of each staff member

Staff roles

Expectations

- Monthly staff meeting

- Ongoing training

Communication

- Chain of command

- Accountability

- Confidentiality

- Staff bulletin boards

- Staff newsletter

- Emails

- Staff suggestion box

Center layout

- Where to park

- Where not to park

- Location of staff entrance

- Location of staff lounge

- Location of storage for staff belongings

- Location of staff bathrooms

Volunteers

- Parents (guidelines, rules, supervision)

- Community members (guidelines, rules, supervision)

- High school and college students (guidelines, rules, supervision)

Outside vendors

- Guidelines

- Rules

- Supervision

Exit conference

- Why is the staff member leaving the center?

- Could the center have implemented anything to convince the staff member to stay?

- How can the center improve?

Remember, you want the new employee to stay and be a productive member of the center. The best way to ensure that this happens is to start out with solid training on the center's policies, procedures, and job expectations. Your new-hire orientation "is a chance to fill in any gaps a new employee may have in knowledge or skills, to address differences in practices between the employee's previous experience and your program, and to ensure that your new employee understands the expectations associated with working in your program," Bergen points out.

"Orientation helps new employees not only learn the specifics of the job but also understand the rules of the road within the program."

After Orientation

Ask the new employee and the mentor to provide you with feedback on the progress of settling into the new job. This way, any undesirable behavior can be addressed quickly, and appropriate performance can be complimented. Feedback from the program director will build the new employee's confidence, and the staff members will feel supported. "Direct and clear feedback, whether positive or not, provides staff members with correct assumptions and teaches them what to expect," assert McGovern and Shelly.

To be effective, workers need direction, encouragement, feedback, and reinforcement. Marvin warns that if program directors allow policies to be broken, tolerate standards being compromised, or fail to act when action is needed, they will lose the respect and support of the staff members. Be certain to outline the consequences of not abiding by the policies and procedures, so that everyone on the staff is aware. "If you need to take corrective action, you should not wait for a formal evaluation but address the issues quickly, clearly following guidelines established in your policies and procedures," Reno, Stutzman, and Zimmerman say. The consequences should be the same for all employees, if you want to maintain trust and respect. The worst thing you can do is not follow the policy with one employee and then enforce the same policy with another. "By orientating new employees to these expectations, you help create a more consistent and ultimately higher-quality program for the children and families you serve," Bergen asserts. Marvin adds, "Workers who do not receive a thorough orientation to your company never fully understand the game or their place in it. Eventually they will quit out of frustration." The program director should demand a high degree of professionalism from her employees. When this goal is achieved, the center will be successful.

CHAPTER 5:

ONGOING PROFESSIONAL DEVELOPMENT

Professional development is designed to help staff members to develop their current skills and to learn new skills, which will assist the staff both in and out of the classroom. A well-trained staff will ultimately provide a safe and nurturing environment for the children and will reduce the number of mistakes that are made within the center. "Orientation will be most effective when it is followed up by planned staff training and ongoing staff communication," Marvin advises.

Create a written professional-development plan for each staff member. You may wonder why the professional-development plan should be individual. It is because your staff members are individuals with different levels of experience and knowledge. Taylor and Stern say, "The kind of training that works best for each person differs from employee to employee. Some staff members work best at online learning, while others recoil from it and prefer old-fashioned classroom interaction." Have each staff member develop a plan for herself, and then add the goals that you feel are important for the staff member. "Cookie-cutter standard training for all staff is invariably less effective because it is more scattershot and not targeted to meet the needs of each employee," say Taylor and Stern.

Write ongoing professional-development plans yearly, with input from the staff. Each plan should outline the number of training hours that are required and the child-development topics that should be addressed. "If the program director uses the job description and focuses on the job's competencies, training is more aligned with what the job actually does and where the staff member needs to grow," say Taylor and Stern. Let the staff members know where and when the training will be held (in the center after hours, during a staff meeting, or off-site). If the training is to take place off-site, tell them whether they will be compensated for this training.

Ongoing professional development is one way to ensure that you are continuing to provide each staff member with ways to improve and learn new ideas. Schedule regular face-to-face meetings to discuss each staff member's individual progress. "Research shows that professionals who participate in ongoing professional development do a better job addressing the needs of young children and supporting their development," Bergen says. Meet quarterly with each staff member to ensure that the trainings meet the goals defined in the professional development plan and that they are being completed. Of course, you can meet more or less frequently, based on the individual needs of the staff member.

Do not assume that the individual has the knowledge base that you have or that you would expect her to have. Just because you have the knowledge and understanding of classroom management and child development does not mean that everyone working at the center has the same knowledge base.

Utilize teachers who have a skill set that can be shared with the other teachers, such as room arrangement or theme ideas. When you allow staff to assist with training, they will have the opportunity to be elevated to a new level. Encourage staff to improve their skill levels through training while also encouraging them to step out of their comfort zone to complete new tasks. If teachers are resistant to additional training because they have done the same activities for the past five years successfully, then promote small changes to keep the staff up to date on the current child development research.

Training can be a big investment. Is it really worth it? Program directors sometimes state that they do not have the time to train the teachers at their centers. My response is to ask, "Do you have the time to address all the mistakes that will occur without training?" The quality of any early childhood program relies heavily on the quality of those who care for the children. Marvin points out, "Failure to train your staff undermines their personal security and delivers a message that they are not very important to the success of your organization. If you don't care, why should they?" Without proper training, teachers will make mistakes that can place children in potentially harmful situations and may not adhere to the proper health and safety precautions.

Furthermore, teachers will not demonstrate the skills needed to provide the developmentally appropriate atmosphere that is necessary for the children's mental and physical growth.

These are a few of the mistakes that can be made by an untrained or undertrained staff member:

- Interacting with other staff and not watching the children to ensure their safety

- Not asking for proper identification before releasing a child from the center

- Leaving children unattended in classrooms, bathrooms, the gym, or outside on the playground

- Giving infants the incorrect bottle

- Not informing parents verbally or in writing when an accident or incident occurs

- Incorrectly documenting medication or administering incorrect medication to children

Ongoing training is so important because a well-trained staff will ultimately provide a safe and nurturing environment for all children and reduce mistakes that are made within the center. Program directors will be ineffective if they let situations go, hoping that the situations will correct themselves in time. The only thing that ignoring a problem does is promote bad habits that are harder to correct in the future. Taylor and Stern add, "When organizations devote time, budgets, and energy to training, it sends a positive message that the business is investing resources into improving the skills of its staff members." Training has been identified as a major component in improving the quality of teachers and programs. Reno, Stutzman, and Zimmerman assert, "The quality of an early childhood program may be affected by many factors. However, a major determinant of the program's quality is the extent to which the knowledge of child development is applied in the program's practices."

Choosing Effective Training

Have you ever heard anyone say that children have changed, that they are not like they used to be? Some things are different about children, especially with the advent of handheld screens and other technology, but what are early childhood teachers implementing to meet the changing needs of the children? Could it be that teachers are not adapting? This is one of the main reasons why ongoing professional development is important, because children are changing and the staff members need individual professional plans to help them adapt to the needs of the children. "Participation in ongoing professional development helps ensure that you keep up with the latest ideas and research findings in your profession," says Bergen. Encourage staff not only to attend workshops and training but also to provide training for their coworkers as part of the center's professional development. Such support is especially beneficial when you have staff members who are taking college courses, because they will have opportunities to share what they are learning in class. "Employees who are interested in their work, engaged, and challenged on a regular basis most often report that they are highly satisfied," say McGovern and Shelly. This type of training can be implemented as part of the monthly staff meeting or at a separate scheduled time.

All sorts of professional development topics are available to explore. Teachers should never stop learning and growing. They should always look for new techniques founded in research.

The program director can work with the teachers and assistant teachers to develop individualized professional development plans. If the state does not have a required number of professional development hours, twenty-four hours of training per year would be sufficient. The professional development plan should address areas that the program director feels would be beneficial for growth and areas where the staff would like to increase their knowledge and skill level. When the program director and staff work together on professional development, the program and children will benefit. Staff can complete the training by attending local and/or national early childhood conferences, as well as online training programs that are provided through an accredited college or university or an online program that has the International Association for Continuing Education and Training (IACET) provider accreditation. Training topics should cover a variety of subjects, including the following:

- Child development

- Activities for transition times

- Classroom arrangements

- Incorporating diversity into the classroom

- Age-appropriate discipline

- Brain development

- Appropriate communication techniques

- Learning centers

- Infant and toddler development

- Assessment tools

- Social and emotional development

- Early literacy

- Science, technology, engineering, and math (STEM) activities

- Working with children who have behavioral issues

- How to partner with parents to address behavioral issues

- Working as part of a team

- Activities for children outside the classroom

You will know that the training was successful when you see staff members implement what they have learned in their classrooms with the children and in their daily work. If you do not see a change in the staff person's work performance, you will know the training was unsuccessful.

Don't forget about your assistant teachers. Training is especially important for assistant teachers entering the early childhood field, because they typically are not required to have any form of training prior to working with children. They will not have experience or formal training in developmentally appropriate practices within the early child-care setting. A new-hire orientation followed by ongoing professional training will provide the resources necessary to reduce mistakes made by unskilled teachers. Assistant teachers should be provided training on the following, at a minimum:

• The curriculum used at the center

• The importance of play in a child's life and learning

• The state licensing requirements

• The policies and procedures of the center

• Feeding and diapering infants and toddlers

• Appropriate care and supervision of children

• Reporting child abuse and neglect, whether suspected or witnessed

• Effectively and appropriately communicating with parents

• Completing the name-to-face process to maintain accurate daily records

• The playground supervision policy

• How to assist the teacher in the classroom with planning and preparing the learning environment in and out of the classroom

• Cleaning procedures

• The importance of teamwork

Lead teachers often complain that their assistant teachers do not have any early childhood background and do not understand what is developmentally appropriate for the children. They complain that the assistant teachers say or do inappropriate things such as the following:

• Saying no frequently when directing the children

• Not engaging the children during free-play activities

• Not interacting with the children outside on the playground

• Not understanding or respecting the children's artwork; changing a child's drawings; telling children to draw their pictures a certain way, thereby eliminating creativity

- Shaming a child who is being toilet trained by saying that her friends are not having accidents in their pants

- Telling a preschooler that she will have to go back to the toddler classroom if she doesn't behave

- Not reading to the children

- Not asking open-ended questions to stimulate conversations with the children

When an assistant teacher is hired, it should not be the lead teacher's responsibility to train the assistant. Lead teachers need to focus on teaching the children; asking them to also take responsibility for training their assistants is not fair. Lead teachers seldom have the time to properly train a new staff member. The program director should be responsible for training the assistant teachers before they begin working in the classroom. This way, when the assistant teachers start working, they can interact with the children in a developmentally appropriate fashion and can follow through efficiently with the planned activities while keeping the children in a safe and appropriate learning environment.

The teacher-assistant trainings should be designed to prepare them for a future opening when a lead teacher leaves the center. Therefore, consider enrolling staff members in the Teacher Education and Compensation Helps (TEACH) scholarship program. The TEACH program will provide the staff members with the opportunity to acquire training and education to become qualified lead caregivers, which will benefit the center. According to Taylor and Stern, "The organization that can hold onto their staff, develop them into leaders, move them up the organization, create a steady flow of talent, and not spend the bulk of their time replacing talent will win." With proper training, the assistant teacher can also temporarily fill in as the lead teacher until a qualified lead can be placed in the position. It is important that the program director develop and implement a replacement plan for lead-teacher positions. You should always have at least one or two individuals working at the center who could take on this major role.

CHAPTER 6:
WORKING WITH A DIVERSE WORKFORCE

Today's workforce is comprised of people of different races, genders, cultures, ages, and physical abilities. The program director is the leader at the center and therefore sets the example for the employees to follow. Consequently, say McGovern and Shelly, it is important for the program director to "recognize and be responsive to the traits and characteristics of each group, while maintaining a productive work environment."

Remember that no one wants or likes to be judged based on his race, gender, culture, age, or physical abilities. "When dealing with cultural differences, the first challenge we face is the tendency to confuse culture and universal traits. Because we are brought up in our own culture, we tend to think that everyone does things the same way and that our behaviors and belief systems are self-explanatory," say Laroche and Yang. The more you learn about different cultures and perspectives, the easier it will be for you to interact with employees from different backgrounds or with different abilities. Laroche and Yang advise: "Stereotyping occurs when we use that information to anticipate . . . behavior and act preemptively. By contrast, if we use the information we have about people and the group they belong to as a way to guide our observation and understanding of their behavior, we are using this information in a constructive manner."

Generational Diversity

Generational diversity, in particular, is creating new challenges for program directors. Because the various generations differ in how they interact with each other, say Rebore and Walmsley, it is important for program directors to be aware of the differences and similarities. According to Susan Eisner, author of the article "Managing Generation Y," early childhood staffs often are made up of people from a range of generations:

- Baby boomers, born 1945–1964

- Generation X, born 1965–1980

- Generation Y (millennials), born 1980–late 1990s

- Generation Z, born 1997 or later

Program directors faced with a variety of generations must be creative with their techniques in interacting with their staff members.

As a program director, strive to be flexible and generate programs that attract the Generation Y and Z populations, while also enticing the baby boomers and Generation X populations to stay at the center. "Many employers are finding that flexible work arrangements are effective in meeting both these challenges," advise Nancy Sutton Bell and Marvin Narz in their article "Meeting the Challenges of Age Diversity in the Workplace." They say that employees, whatever their generation, appreciate an employer who provides accommodations that motivate them to achieve greater success in their personal and professional lives. McGovern and Shelly add that program directors "who oversee multiple generations must learn to anticipate the differences they are sure to encounter and not to be offended by any one style of communication." Staff members of different generations will communicate differently, which is expected and acceptable. It is the program director's responsibility to ensure that the staff members are respectful of each other.

Baby Boomers

Baby boomers are not likely to view employment as their identity, assert Kristie Roberts and colleagues, authors of "Strategic Human Resources and Human Capital Development." Baby boomers "created the notion of the workaholic, and sometimes struggle with not seeing their younger coworkers working around the clock," say Corey Seemiller and Meghan Grace, authors of *Generation Z: A Century in the Making*. They use networking to advance their careers. Baby boomers "value . . . interaction with other workers through meetings and 'face time,'" say McGovern and Shelly. Eisner points out that baby boomers are ambitious, and they gauge success through material possessions. They often look for harmony and are willing to compromise;

however, they tend to have an aversion to authoritarianism and laziness, Eisner adds. "Baby [b]oomers can be a volatile substance when mixed with younger generations, who tend to view them as workaholics who value long hours over productivity and creativity," warn McGovern and Shelly. "The [b]oomers' mix of respect and mistrust for technology can alienate younger workers, who have never known life without the internet." Baby boomers are more inclined to use the phone to call for information, but they have embraced email and text messages.

Generation X

At a population of 55 million, Generation X has fewer members than the baby boomers (76 million) or the millennials (62 million), according to Richard Fry's article for the Pew Research Center. Born at a time of increasing divorce rates and higher maternal participation in the workforce, they experienced less adult supervision than previous generations. Left to themselves, they became independent and resourceful, says Sally Kane in her article "The Common Characteristics of Generation X Professionals." Not surprisingly, they tend to be independent workers. The Generation X population is not eager to work as part of a team; they prefer to complete tasks on their own. They do not require or desire a great deal of direction. Instead, they desire instant feedback from the lead teacher or program director and prefer a coaching management style. Generation X tends to think outside the box, and they are not focused on longevity within the center. They tend to find security in their skill set and are continuously working to acquire new skills. According to Eisner, the Generation X population is "likely to value developing skills more than gaining job titles. They do not take well to micromanaging." Members of Generation X generally are not willing to work long hours, and they have the desire to balance work and family. This generation tends to work faster and smarter and is not concerned with breaking the rules to achieve desired goals in a timely fashion.

Generation Y (Millennials)

The Generation Y population, generally referred to as millennials, is motivated by work environments that make sense. According to Bell and

Narz, they desire jobs that promote flexibility, telecommuting options, and the ability to work part time or to leave the workforce temporarily when having children. Millennials also require a work environment that holds their attention and is interesting and enjoyable. "They generally work well in teams," say Rebore and Walmsley, "and they like constant feedback. They like to plan for the future and take a genuine interest in the organization for which they work." Millennials desire a work environment that generates innovative challenges and projects with deadlines that promote ownership of their tasks. Furthermore, they will "frequently seek and expect positive reinforcement for their work," assert McGovern and Shelly. Millennials will not maintain employment with a company for the paycheck as previous generations will. They tend to have a high regard for professional development and are determined to work faster and better because they can multitask.

Generation Z, the Post-Millennials

Members of Generation Z are just starting to enter the work force. They are dedicated to their employer, and they want to make a difference in the world. "This is a generation that wants to come home at the end of the day feeling good about what they contributed to the world through their work," say Seemiller and Grace. Therefore, they take their jobs seriously and are not eager to change jobs when they are feeling valued. "It will be important for employers if they want to retain this generation of workers to help them see a path to their futures, especially within the organization," Seemiller and Grace assert. Time will tell how this generation will affect the workforce. "Given their open-mindedness and diverse social circles, those in Generation Z seek a workplace that is similarly diverse. They see the value of differences and know that diversity is what makes organizations stronger," Seemiller and Grace say.

Conflict between the generations can be resolved when staff members recognize that each generation has a different yet important perspective, which, when respected, will be beneficial to the children and themselves. Often, conflicts occur when a staff person who has been teaching for many years feels that his approach is working and is not open to the changes that the younger generations suggest. For example, a baby boomer likes the way he arranges his classroom; he's been doing it the same way for years. A millennial or Generation

Z employee wants to rearrange the classroom to reduce discipline problems. In such as case, the younger employee could suggest implementing the proposed classroom arrangement for a month to see if the discipline problems are reduced. Compromise is good, and when it comes to changing a baby boomer's mind, tangible evidence works best. This way, both staff members feel respected and validated.

Differences in communication styles can also cause conflict. The baby boomer generation will often speak to millennials or members of Generation Z as if they are children rather than adults and colleagues. The millennials and Generation Z employees can become offended by the baby boomers. This conflict can be resolved by baby boomers recognizing their colleagues as equals who are not children and who deserve to be treated with respect. On the other hand, it is important for millennial and Generation Z employees to be professional while at work to show that they are committed to the center and the program. Millennials and Generation Z employees may have a difficult time speaking up to the baby boomer employees because they do not want to appear disrespectful.

The best way to resolve conflict between the generations is to respect each other and the value that they each bring to the center and the children. Remember that because you are working together at a child-care center, the most important thing that you have in common is the desire to create a healthy learning environment for children, and that is where you start when conflict arises. It is important to focus on what you have in common, discuss the things that you agree with and the items that you can agree to disagree on, and then outline the steps to follow. Together, decide what can be negotiated to make the work environment positive and productive for everyone. Develop a joint plan to address and resolve the conflict. If the children's best interest is the priority, then an agreement can be reached without major conflict. Conflict is not resolved by talking to other coworkers about the situation or having the program director address the concerns. Only speaking with the individual can solve the situation without incident. Involving coworkers will only make the conflict more complicated.

Cultural Diversity

Laroche and Yang say that "cultural differences are based on the fact that people in one country are taught to behave in a certain way in a given situation, while people in another country are taught to behave in a different way in the same situation." When program directors take the time to learn about the different cultures of their staff members, they will have a better understanding of how to communicate in an effective manner, which will be beneficial for everyone. Charlene Solomon and Michael Schell, authors of *Managing Across Cultures*, advise self-awareness: "By understanding what culture is, how you've been shaped by your own culture, and how your cultural values differ from those of people in other parts of the world, you can become more perceptive and successful."

Recognize that staff members may have the same background yet respond differently. Solomon and Schell say that "no two people from a culture are exactly the same, so recognizing national characteristics isn't enough. Within every culture, individuals have their own personal styles and behavioral preferences that represent the diversity in that culture." Program directors should create an environment within the center that is accepting and supportive of different cultures. Laroche and Yang agree, advising that staff be required "to strive to understand each other's perspectives in order to leverage the strengths of these different perspectives." This will make the center a supportive work environment for all employees.

When individuals from different backgrounds work together, they will see situations differently and have different approaches to problem solving as well as to promoting change within the center. "When you work with culturally different people, there will be times when you find yourself feeling offended, annoyed, or disrespected. Keep in mind that this does not imply that they mean to make you feel this way. Since you may interpret their message differently from what they mean, you first need to monitor your own emotions and realize when you are reacting negatively," Laroche and Yang advise. Having different perspectives will benefit the center. To effectively lead change and foster an inclusive culture at the center, Laroche and Yang say that the program director needs to recognize and acknowledge that people from different parts of the world want change to happen differently. Furthermore, there is not a right or wrong way when it comes to different points of view. The important factor is that everyone has an opinion. Everyone should be allowed to voice their points of view, and their opinions should be valued. When individuals feel respected and valued, they will be willing to stay at the center longer than staff members that do not feel connected or valued.

For example, let's say that a disagreement arises when one teacher observes and voices a difference in how she handles feeding, when compared to her coteacher. She suggests that the coteacher change her practice and offers reasons why. The coteacher interprets what was intended as a topic for discussion as judgment that she does not know her job. The first teacher is accustomed to being direct and open, and the other is more accustomed to a less direct tone and approach. This can be resolved by the two teachers sitting down and discussing their individual interpretations of the approach used.

When conflict arises, speak with the individual in a respectful manner, state the facts of the situation, talk about the behavior—not the individual's personality— and explain how the situation made you feel and how it could be handled differently going forward. Listen to the individual with the purpose of understanding. It is important when working with individuals from different cultures that you take the time to share and learn how you both will respond and react to situations so that a mutual respect can be formed.

CHAPTER 7:
HANDLING STAFF
TURNOVER

I like Bill Marvin's description of *staff turnover*, outlined in his book *From Turnover to Teamwork:* "Losing staff members you did not want to lose when you did not expect to lose them, and staff members who abandon their jobs or leave with less than two weeks' notice." Reno, Stutzman, and Zimmerman report that a 2003 study on job turnover and occupational turnover among child-care center educators and directors found that child-care centers had the highest turnover rate in the care and education field. Quality-of-life issues are becoming more important, as workers realize there is more to happiness than just money. Program directors who do not provide a healthy work/life balance for their staff members will ultimately experience a higher staff turnover. Because people are working to make a living, they must have some time to live. Marvin warns that if your staff members do not have time to spend with their families, are unable to take a day off when they need it, or are burning themselves out routinely, they will eventually find another job.

Some individuals will start looking for a new job within the first week of employment if they are not satisfied. McGovern and Shelly go so far as to say, "The fact is that many employees are always looking for the next position." When a staff member leaves the center, the remaining staff members are often overworked to fill the void. Staff turnover can produce problems for the whole program. If a staff member leaves after a short stay, it can potentially cost the center financially for a new job search. Taylor and Stern add, "In addition, it can trigger morale issues because of the early exit." Recognize that "all turnover is a management problem, either because management failed to provide a productive working environment or because the wrong person was hired in the first place," Marvin says.

If a center is experiencing high staff turnover, the program director will frequently blame the staff member who decides to leave, saying that she just wanted more than what the center could pay or that the staff member was not a good worker. Although these descriptions may be accurate in some situations, they are not the main reason that a center experiences high staff turnover. Marvin asserts, "Survey results indicate that salary, benefits, and job security are less important to most workers than appreciation and involvement. While pay should be at or above the going rate in your market for positions of similar skill and authority, high wages alone will not be enough to keep good workers if the working conditions and quality of supervision is substandard."

Program directors have to recognize that staff members will leave a center that lacks opportunities for upward mobility, has vague job descriptions, lacks leadership, has poor management, and lacks teamwork. Program directors who do not value their employees or have not built a working relationship with the staff members are likely to see staff turnover. When staff members are at a center with high staff turnover, they will question why they are staying and, as a result, they may leave. They likely have watched so many of their coworkers depart, without the program director working actively to encourage staff to stay, that they will leave if they cannot come up with a good reason to stay—not necessarily because they are personally having any issues at the center.

When a center has a high staff-turnover rate, the program director will have a hard time operating the program. Spending the majority of the time recruiting, hiring, and training new staff takes away from the time that the director has to promote the center to recruit new families. She will thus find herself on a treadmill, running in place instead of moving the center forward. Such a situation is frustrating for everyone, say McGovern and Shelly. Moreover, parents do not like to see different staff members interacting with their children. Having high turnover rates, according to Rhodes and Huston, can lower the quality of care provided to the children in the program because frequent staff changes can have a negative effect on the children's development. This is particularly true for infants and toddlers, because consistent primary care is so important for their development. Their attachment is disrupted every time there is a new staff member introduced into their classroom.

While it's not realistic for program directors to think that they will never lose a staff member, keeping staff turnover to a minimum is in everyone's best interest, McGovern and Shelly assert. Reduce staff turnover by, obviously, hiring the right person for the position. Also, recognize and support staff for the skills that they bring to the position. The program director should have a clear set of expectations and explain and maintain them with all employees. "The key to ensuring low turnover is to keep employees engaged and interested in their jobs and to create some incentives for them to want to stay," advise McGovern and Shelly.

On the other hand, not all staff turnover is bad. "Some turnover is healthy. You want a natural flow of people moving into the organization who bring new skills, and employees moving out of the organization who may want to switch careers or transition into new challenges, or whose performance reviews suggest that they are not your highly motivated and skilled employees," say Taylor and Stern. Staff members choose to leave for many reasons:

- Graduating from high school or college

- Moving out of the area

- Having or adopting a child

- Being diagnosed with a medical condition

- Caring for a family member

- Finding a job in a different field

- Finding a new job within the same field

- Transferring to another location

- Retirement

Recognize that everyone on your staff will eventually leave the center. Most will provide two weeks' notice when they choose to go. Marvin points out that this "shows that they have respect for, and feel some identity with, the organization."

Not all staff choose to leave on their own. In the case of terminating a staff member's employment, Taylor and Stern say, "It is classic tomfoolery to focus on retaining staff members who should have never made it into the center in the first place. If you hire the wrong people and then hold onto them, they could cause the center to fail." When staff members are not performing well, terminating their employment is necessary.

The program director should review the recruiting and hiring procedures to see if the correct candidates are being hired. Reviewing the training process to see if the staff members are provided with the tools to succeed in the position is also crucial. An exit conference can be beneficial in learning about staff members' perceptions of the center and the reasons why staff leave. If program directors are not willing to consider the role that they play when an employee leaves, whether voluntarily or involuntarily, then the turnover cycle will continue.

The exit conference can be the first step in fixing the problem. If you are having a hard time retaining staff, take the time to evaluate why by completing an exit conference with each staff member who leaves the center. If, at the exit conference, you are only hearing that staff are dissatisfied, then there is a major disconnect. Ask the staff member questions such as the following:

- What can or should be done to improve the center?

- Why are you leaving the center?

- What improvements could or should be made to improve the program for the children and families?

- What would you have liked to know about the center when you were hired that was not explained to you?

- What could or should be done to improve staff interactions?

"The most important takeaway from exit interviews is to elicit information from the staff member and then act on it," advise Taylor and Stern.

According to Marvin, staff members are most likely to be leaving because of something the program director did or allowed to happen, or because the program director did not listen to them while they were employed. Listen with an open mind, and be willing to address the person's concerns. Marvin advises that, if the staff member is reluctant to talk directly with you, you should consider hiring someone outside the center to conduct the exit interview. This person should be someone who is safe to talk to and who will respect confidentiality. Or, have the exiting staff member complete an online exit interview. The only downside to online surveys is that you cannot ask follow-up questions that may be helpful. After completing the exit interview, it is the program director's responsibility to make any necessary changes. We will explore ways to do that in the next chapter.

CHAPTER 8:
RETAINING THE BEST PERSON FOR THE POSITION

After all your hard work finding, hiring, and training your center staff, you will want to keep them for as long as possible. It is important to retain the staff for continuity of the program and stability for the children and families who attend the center. Remember, parents do not like change. And when a teacher leaves, children will have to adjust to a new teacher with a potentially different teaching style. It is important to invest time and energy into retaining staff members who are productive and who help provide a quality environment for the children and families at the center. Retaining the best person for the position, however, does not mean that you should keep every employee who is hired. "Without some influx of new talent and ideas, it is easy for an operation to get stale. The goal of a successful retention program is not zero turnover," Marvin asserts. The goal is to retain the best staff members for the center. This chapter will provide practical ways to retain the right staff members for your center. To improve staff retention, consider the following:

- Keep an open mind.

- Do not micromanage.

- Maintain an open-door policy to generate open communication.

- Nurture relationships.

- Provide training.

- Respond to staff members' needs.

- Set clear expectations.

- Address the reasons for job dissatisfaction.

Keep an Open Mind

When staff members come to you with a new idea or concern, listen to them. Whenever possible, implement their ideas and always address their concerns. When you are unable to implement their ideas for various reasons, such as financial or staffing challenges, always explain that the ideas are welcomed but they may not be implemented. That way, your employees know that their ideas are valued. Feeling valued is important when it comes to retaining staff.

Do Not Micromanage

When you have selected and hired the best candidate for the position, provide a comprehensive new-hire orientation that outlines the center's requirements of the position and the expectations of the management. With this in place, micromanagement will be unnecessary. Allow the staff member to do the job that he was hired for. When program directors micromanage their staff, they are sending the message that they do not trust the judgment of the staff and therefore have to make sure that staff are implementing their jobs appropriately. Staff members, especially ones with years of experience and training, are unlikely to stay in a job where this occurs.

Maintain an Open-Door Policy to Generate Open Communication

"Open communication is the key to effectiveness for any organization. It becomes even more important for multicultural organizations because there are a thousand and one ways culturally different people can misunderstand one another, even when everyone involved has the best intentions," Laroche and Yang advise. Recognize and make the most of staff members within their areas of expertise. Support your staff when needed, treat everyone with respect, and be an effective communicator and good listener.

Nurture Relationships

Recognize that retaining the best staff members is a key factor in building your dream team. As Taylor and Stern put it, "When retention is given the same respect as recruiting, the odds are strong that you will hold on to a much higher percentage of your staff members." Get to know your staff members, and invest in them in a way that makes them feel appreciated.

Early childhood professionals want to be heard, valued, respected, and treated fairly. Recognize that, "just as teachers build relationships with children in order to best support their learning and development, program directors must build relationships with teachers to best foster professional growth. Doing so will also establish trust, a necessary element in a caring community," says Angèle Sancho Passe, author of *Evaluating and Supporting Early Childhood Teachers*. Marvin also points out that "people naturally feel more secure and perform better in a supportive work climate." They want to work at a center that is professional, where all staff members are treated fairly. The program director should not show favoritism or enforce rules inconsistently. According to Taylor and Stern, "Treating them with respect, being on time, listening to them, asking them questions, and responding quickly to their questions are all ways to establish a relationship with them that can turn into long-term employees." Therefore, the better the staff members are treated, the more likely they are to stay at the center, especially if they feel that the program director is taking the time to invest in them.

Create strong individual relationships with your staff. "Most people change jobs, not because they are seeking more money but because of dissatisfaction with their bosses," say Taylor and Stern. While this may be true in some cases, many individuals will stay in their positions because of the relationship that they have with their direct supervisor or the program director.

Provide Training

Ongoing training is one of the most important things you can do to retain your staff. The quality of the center is the direct result of the caliber of the people who work there. Encourage your staff members to step out of their comfort zones and develop new skills. When training your staff, outline expectations, provide positive feedback along with areas for improvement, demonstrate positive behavior, encourage staff members to work both independently and as a team, and provide direction when needed.

Will training teachers and assistant teachers reduce mistakes? The answer is yes—training can drastically reduce the number of mistakes that can occur at a center. Training will also make the teachers accountable for their actions. After you have provided training, have the staff sign a form stating that they have been trained on the information provided and that they understand they are now being held accountable. This will also serve as your documentation that the training was provided.

Respond to Staff Members' Needs

Just as you would individualize the training required for your staff, you should individualize your strategies for keeping staff members at the center. "What will make the applicant stay at the job is just as important as whether the applicant possesses the skills to do the job," say Taylor and Stern. For each employee, create a written plan with goals and objectives to encourage growth. Consider the needs of each staff member, as well. For example, one staff member may need to start work after 9:00 a.m., so that he can get his children to school. Another may need to leave at 3:30 p.m. for an evening class. Yet another staff member may need to take an elderly parent to visit a doctor occasionally. Having a flexible schedule for some staff members may be the factor that outweighs the appeal of another center that pays the same but does not allow flexibility with scheduling.

Set Clear Expectations

Set clear expectations for all employees, and explain and enforce them consistently. Coach and mentor staff members to build their skill levels. Model the behavior that you expect from them, and be consistent. Encourage teamwork. Marvin advises that "the path from turnover to teamwork is simply a matter of creating and maintaining a nurturing work environment. In that type of climate, insecurity diminishes, and people are free to do their jobs." Recognize that when you hire the right person for the position and provide the needed training, the chances of that person staying at the center are higher. According to Taylor and Stern, "If the boss isn't skilled at building trust or developing a climate that challenges and supports people, employees leave." Ensure that staff members are trained on the center's policies and procedures and that they understand the expectations of their positions.

Address the Reasons for Job Dissatisfaction

Of course, there are individuals who will start looking for a new job within the first week of employment and will leave if they are not satisfied with their position for any reason. If a staff member is dissatisfied with the center or with his position, you need to recognize and understand the reasons. The following are a few of the more common reasons people leave a job:

- Lack of direction or vague direction

- Inconsistent job responsibilities

- Lack of teamwork

- Lack of training

- Low pay

Are staff members leaving the center because they do not feel appreciated or part of the team? If this is the case, it is the responsibility of the program director to build a team environment by creating a supportive atmosphere. Recognize that staff members will not stay at a center where they feel that they are treated poorly or where they are not appreciated. If you invest the time to find the root of the problem, then you can correct the situation and reduce staff turnover. "The primary intent of a retention program is to be sure you don't lose your truly great workers—the achievers and the keepers—unexpectedly," explains Marvin. Listen carefully to find out why staff members are leaving the center, and correct the situation.

Steps to Address Dissatisfied Staff

When you're confronted with a dissatisfied staff member, here are steps you can take to address the situation:

- Provide motivation.

- Offer a raise or bonus.

- Offer nonmonetary incentives.

- Provide leadership opportunities and responsibility.

- Recognize achievement and hard work.

- Offer a promotion.

Motivation

Motivation is encouraging someone to accomplish something that he may not have the desire to complete. Although some individuals do not require motivation to complete a task, a majority of employees do require some form of motivation. The key to motivating a diverse staff is to understand and acknowledge their individual differences and to understand how each person is motivated. Stephen Robbins, David DeCenzo, and Robert Wolter, authors of *Supervision Today!*, say that you cannot assume that the same techniques will motivate all employees because motivational concepts are not always universal. For example, program directors should not try to motivate a college student in the same fashion in which they would a seasoned employee.

Motivation may be based on many different factors, such as culture, race, gender, or generational differences. Ultimately, program directors who know their staff members individually will know what each requires to be motivated. One employee may be motivated by more vacation days. Another may be motivated by a raise, and yet another may be motivated by a promotion or new title.

Program directors must also recognize the differences between the generations. Baby boomers can be motivated by being told that they are competent and doing a good job, so offer regular feedback on their job performance. Members of Generation X, on the other hand, desire to be allowed to complete tasks in their own manner, because they tend to think outside the box. The Generation X population does not take pleasure in excessive rules and regulation. Generation Y can be motivated by being part of a team. "Supervisors must be flexible enough in their supervisory style to seek the involvement of all employees and be aware of the fact that all employees are differently motivated in terms of what they want and need from work," advise Robbins, DeCenzo, and Wolter.

Raises and Bonuses

Staff members should be paid a fair wage for their position. That said, provide them with raises whenever possible. This will let them know that you care about their financial stability. The raise should be provided after a year of service and, at a minimum, annually thereafter. While additional funds are always nice to have, the raise will mean more when it is attached to performance. Individuals will not appreciate receiving the same raise as the person who is always late to work and is not a team player; there is no incentive to be a top performer if everyone is receiving the same raise at the same time. Also consider offering bonuses. According to Marvin, when it comes to monetary rewards, a bonus is usually better than a raise, especially when the reward is tied directly to behavior.

Nonmonetary Incentives

There are lots of ways to show your appreciation for hard work. You can send a card, a small gift, or a gift card to the employee's home. A simple "thank you" also goes a long way in showing the employee that she is valued. Offer an additional vacation day as recognition for going above and beyond. Acknowledge extra effort with praise.

Have special treats for staff during staff meetings, or organize a staff appreciation day. If possible, ask a local restaurant to donate the food. If you cannot find a restaurant to donate, ask if they could provide the food at a discounted price. Then you can allow the restaurant to advertise at your center in return.

Incorporate activities such as a holiday party or a yearly summer or fall outing for staff and their families, to show that you value your employees' hard work. This allows staff members to create relationships outside of the center and to see each other in a nonwork situation. "The goal is to regularly share a laugh with your staff and give them stories to tell others," says Marvin. Laroche and Yang advise, "Organize events and create opportunities to encourage employees to build good working relationships with their colleagues."

Leadership Responsibility

Taylor and Stern say that "developing talent is one of the keys to retaining people and filling future slots internally." Even if you can't promote an employee, you can still allow her to take on a leadership role if she is excelling in the tasks she already has. Find ways that your employees can begin to lead, which may not always mean that they are taking responsibilities away from you.

During staff meetings, have the staff brainstorm responses to "What would you add or change at the center if money were no object?" This will allow everyone the opportunity to think outside the box. Your staff will probably offer suggestions that can be implemented with the funds that the center already has. When a teacher's idea is implemented, she will feel appreciated and valued, which is what many staff members want from the program director. "One of the simplest and most effective morale boosters a manager can employ is to make sure that employees feel appreciated," advise McGovern and Shelly.

Encourage your staff to move into leadership positions, even if those positions are not at your center. Provide them with the tools to be able to move up if they decide to leave; train them to be program directors. The skills that you are providing will create another quality program for children and families, which will have a positive impact on the early childhood field. As a program director, you should never be afraid to give your teachers more responsibility or to provide them with additional skills for fear that they will take your position away from you. If you are the best at your job, you have no reason to worry about being replaced, because your supervisor wants you to stay. Consider too that you may want to move on one day, and who better to take your place than one of the teachers you have trained?

Recognition

As McGovern and Shelly point out, "Recognition programs are important, there's no question about it. An employee will work for a paycheck, but an employee who is recognized and rewarded for particular jobs will work happily and productively, with greater motivation than the weekly or biweekly check." Have the staff create a list of the criteria for choosing an employee of the month or quarter. Allow the staff to choose the employee; set out a tamperproof voting box or use an online voting system. Allowing the staff to determine the employee of the month or quarter reduces the chance of their feeling as if you are playing favorites. Tip: The same employee should not be selected two months in a row. If you find that the same few people are always being named, then it's time to change the criteria.

Promotion

Develop your staff talent and hire from within whenever possible. Hiring assistant teachers who are in college pursuing an early childhood or child development degree will make it easier to promote from within the center when an opening occurs. If your assistants are not enrolled in an early childhood program, encourage them to take classes or begin a child development associate (CDA) program. Promoting from within the program will let the assistant teachers know that you are invested in their growth and careers.

Conclusion

The overall goal for the center is to provide a safe and nurturing environment for the children. This will be accomplished by building a dream team through the recruiting, hiring, training, and retaining efforts that will place the right staff member into the right position. Each step in the process is equally important to the overall function of the center. Incorporate a strong recruiting and hiring procedure, follow up with new-hire training and ongoing training, and review and evaluate each process regularly. This way, you will create and maintain consistency with the dream team that you have worked so hard to build.

Appendix A: Sample Application-Review Form

Candidate Name: _____

Position: Lead Teacher, Infant/Toddler classroom

Date of Interview: _____

Education (check one):

☐ Bachelor's degree or higher in early childhood education or child development (25 pts.)

☐ Bachelor's degree or higher in a child-related field (20 pts.)

☐ Associate's degree in child development (15 pts.)

☐ Associate's degree in a child-related field (10 pts.)

☐ Current CDA (7 pts.)

☐ Semester hours without a degree (5 pts.)

☐ High school diploma/GED (2 pts.)

Years of experience in early childhood education (check one):

☐ 10 or more years (25 pts.) ☐ 5–10 years (20 pts.)

☐ 3–5 years (10 pts.) ☐ 2–3 years (7 pts.)

☐ 1–2 years (5 pts.) ☐ Less than a year (2 pts.)

Specialty (check one):

☐ Infant/Toddler semester hours with CDA (25 pts.)

☐ Infant/Toddler CDA without semester hours (20 pts.)

☐ Infant/Toddler semester hours without CDA (15 pts.)

Years of infant/toddler experience (check one):

☐ 10 or more years (25 pts.) ☐ 5–10 years (20 pts.)

☐ 3–5 years (10 pts.) ☐ 2–3 years (7 pts.)

☐ 1–2 years (5 pts.) ☐ Less than a year (2 pts.)

Total points: _____

Appendix B: Sample Post-Interview Assessment Form

Name _____

Position Lead Teacher

Date of Interview _____

Skill Set	Demonstrated (10 points)	Partially Demonstrated (5 points)	Needs Improvement (3 points)	Did Not Demonstrate (0 points)
Has the ability to communicate effectively				
Has the appropriate education for the position				
Understands child development				
Written portion is clear and concise with minimal to no spelling errors				
Effective problem-solving skills				
Demonstrates the ability to take initiative				
Has appropriate training for the position				
Demonstrates skills that are beneficial for the position				
Ability to lead a classroom				
Effective conflict-resolution skills				
Demonstrates understanding of the curriculum				
Total				

Appendix C: Sample Pretest/Posttest for New Classroom Employees

Answer true (T) or false (F) to the following statements.

_____ Play is spontaneous and voluntary at the center.

_____ Teachers should interact with each other more than with the children in the classroom.

_____ Play fulfills a wide variety of purposes in a child's life.

_____ Teachers should yell across the classroom to get the children's attention.

_____ Play stimulates a child's imagination.

_____ Parallel play is not important for children, and children should always be engaged with each other.

_____ Teachers should model appropriate behavior in the classrooms with the children.

_____ Play is universal for all children.

_____ You can leave the children unattended if you have to leave the classroom for any reason.

_____ Teachers should not interact with the children while they are playing.

_____ Free play is not important.

_____ A name-to-face head count is required before leaving the classroom.

_____ You are not required to greet parents when they arrive.

_____ If a child is injured, you are not required to report the injury.

_____ You are a mandated reporter.

_____ Anyone can pick up a child with proper identification.

_____ When the children are outside on the playground, it is a break time for the teacher.

Answer the following questions.

What is the adult-child ratio for each age group? _____

What is a blind spot in the classroom? _____

_____

Why are blind spots bad in the classroom? _____

_____

What is the process for calling in sick? _____

_____

How would you report an injury that occurred at the center? _____

_____

What are the center's philosophy and mission statement? _____

_____

Does the center have a dress code? _____

_____

If yes, please describe the dress code. _____

_____

What is the social-media policy? _____

_____

Are cell phones allowed in the classroom? _____

_____

If you observe staff being inappropriate with children, are you required to
report the incident? If so, to whom? _____

_____

Are the children allowed to leave the classroom without adult supervision?

_____

What are the training requirements? _____

_____

How are days off requested? _____

_____

References

American Academy of Pediatrics. 2016. "SIDS and Other Sleep-Related Infant Deaths: Updated 2016 Recommendations for a Safe Infant Sleeping Environment." *Pediatrics* 138(5). https://pediatrics.aappublications.org/content/138/5/e20162938

American Association of Neurological Surgeons. n.d. "Shaken Baby Syndrome." American Association of Neurological Surgeons. https://www.aans.org/Patients/Neurosurgical-Conditions-and-Treatments/Shaken-Baby-Syndrome

American Heart Association. n.d. "Find a CPR Course." American Heart Association https://cpr.heart.org/en

American Red Cross. n.d. "Find a First Aid Training Class." American Red Cross. https://www.redcross.org/take-a-class/first-aid

Barber, Alison E. 1998. *Recruiting Employees: Individual and Organizational Perspectives*. Thousand Oaks, CA: Sage.

Bell, Nancy Sutton, and Marvin Narz. 2007. "Meeting the Challenges of Age Diversity in the Workplace." *The CPA Journal* 56–60. http://archives.cpajournal.com/2007/207/essentials/p56.htm

Bergen, Sharon. 2016. *Early Childhood Staff Orientation Guide*. St. Paul, MN: Redleaf.

Bloodborne Pathogen Training. n.d. "What Is Bloodborne Pathogen Training?" Bloodborne Pathogen Training. https://www.bloodbornepathogentraining.com/

Centers for Disease Control and Prevention. n.d. "Basic TB Facts." Centers for Disease Control and Prevention. https://www.cdc.gov/tb/topic/basics/default.htm

Chambers, Harry E. 2001. *Finding, Hiring, and Keeping Peak Performers: Every Manager's Guide*. Cambridge, MA: Perseus.

ChildCare.gov. n.d. "Background Checks: What You Need to Know." ChildCare.gov https://www.childcare.gov/consumer-education/background-checks-what-you-need-to-know

Cooper, Dominic, Ivan T. Robertson, and Gordon Tinline. 2003. *Recruitment and Selection: A Framework for Success*. London, UK: Cengage.

Eisner, Susan P. 2005. "Managing Generation Y." *SAM Advanced Management Journal* 70(4): 4–15.

Fader, Sunny, and Angela Erickson. 2017. *365 Ideas for Recruiting, Retaining, Motivating, and Rewarding Your Volunteers: A Complete Guide for Nonprofit Organizations*. 2nd edition. Ocala, FL: Atlantic.

Fry, Richard. 2018. "Millennials Projected to Overtake Baby Boomers as America's Largest Generation." Pew Research Center. https://www.pewresearch.org/fact-tank/2018/03/01/millennials-overtake-baby-boomers/

Kane, Sally. 2019. "The Common Characteristics of Generation X Professionals." The Balance Careers. https://www.thebalancecareers.com/common-characteristics-of-generation-x-professionals-2164682

Laroche, Lionel, and Caroline Yang. 2014. *Danger and Opportunity: Bridging Culture and Diversity for Competitive Advantage*. New York, NY: Routledge.

Marvin, Bill. 1994. *From Turnover to Teamwork: How to Build and Retain a Customer-Oriented Foodservice Staff*. New York, NY: John Wiley and Sons.

McGovern, Julia, and Susan Shelly. 2008. *The Happy Employee: 101 Ways for Managers to Attract, Retain, and Inspire the Best and Brightest*. Avon, MA: Adams Business.

National Health and Safety Association. n.d. "Our Mission: Painless Training." National Health and Safety Association. https://www.cpr.io/about/

Rebore, Ronald W., and Angela L. E. Walmsley. 2010. *Recruiting and Retaining Generation Y Teachers*. Thousand Oaks, CA: Corwin.

Reno, Hilde, Janet Stutzman, and Judy Zimmerman. 2008. *Handbook for Early Childhood Administrators: Directing with a Mission*. Boston, MA: Pearson Education.

Rhodes, Holly, and Aletha Huston. 2012. "Building the Workforce Our Youngest Children Deserve." *Society for Research in Child Development Social Policy Report* 26(1): 1–31.

Robbins, Stephen P., David A. DeCenzo, and Robert M. Wolter. 2019. *Supervision Today!* 9th edition. New York, NY: Pearson

Roberts, Kristie, et al. 2008. "Strategic Human Resources and Human Capital Development: Strategies for Managing the 21st Century Workforce." *Forum on Public Policy: A Journal of the Oxford Round Table.* Summer: 1–9.

Sancho Passe, Angèle. 2015. *Evaluating and Supporting Early Childhood Teachers.* St. Paul, MN: Redleaf.

Seemiller, Corey, and Meghan Grace. 2019. *Generation Z: A Century in the Making.* New York, NY: Routledge.

Solomon, Charlene M., and Michael S. Schell. 2009. *Managing Across Cultures: The Seven Keys to Doing Business with a Global Mindset.* New York, NY: McGraw Hill.

Taylor, Johnny C., Jr., and Gary M. Stern, Jr. 2009. *The Trouble with HR: An Insider's Guide to Finding and Keeping the Best Talent.* New York, NY: American Management Association.

United States Department of Labor, Occupational Health and Safety Administration. 2012. 1910.1030 Bloodborne Pathogens. Occupational Health and Safety Administration Standards. https://www.osha.gov/laws-regs/regulations/standardnumber/1910/1910.1030

Index

Build Your Dream Team